Mindfulness for Kids

Jasmine Warren

I

ISBN-13: 978-1979839358

ISBN-10: 1979839352

DEDICATION

For my kids.

CONTENTS

ACKNOWLEDGMENTS

With thanks to my publishers, who were a constant support.

1 INTRODUCING MINDFULNESS

Sometimes our children do peculiar actions, ask peculiar questions and say peculiar things, but they are new to a world that we've lived in for decades. As parents, it's our responsibility to teach our children the skills they need to move forward and live a happy, healthy life. But why mindfulness?

Every day we take for granted the life that we live, the things that we experience and the way we feel. We don't always take the time to be present or to accept the conflicting and negative emotions we feel, and it's likely our children do the same. Our children mimic our habits, our words, and even our emotional responses – they learn from us and follow our lead.

One day my daughter and I were visiting the park, and she had filled a castle bucket full of mud and dirt. She had spent quite a while gathering together the yellow sand at the top, the white sand on the sides, and the mud in the center. When she was finally ready, she flipped over the castle and turned to look at me, hoping that I was watching all the effort she had put in and could see her beautiful castle. Right as she turned to look at me, another child tripped and collapsed part of her castle.

I was horrified because I knew my daughter. She was going to be so angry – she's the temperamental kind, the bossy "takes no lip from anyone" type of girl – and she would not have let that boy get away with ruining her masterpiece. I was over there faster than a kid chasing an ice-cream truck, and snatched her up before she could do any damage to the boy. She was furious; she looked at me with the most cross face ever, and when I tried to tell her it was an accident she wouldn't listen. So instead of allowing her anger to anger me, I picked her up and made her focus on breathing and not on her anger. She was resistant and hard-headed at first, but soon she unconsciously began to breathe with me. I watched our chests rise and lower in conjunction.

When we were done breathing, I set her down and told her to be nice. The once furious expression was now just a regular goofy grin, as she strolled over to the boy who fell and asked him if he was okay. He told her he was fine, and then he offered to help her fix her castle. She was thrilled – probably because she likes having assistants and being the boss. Regardless, her first experience at mindfulness was a success. Talk about being a proud mommy! I had only just decided to actually attempt mindfulness with my daughter the day before – I vowed that the next opportunity presented to me would be snatched up with fervor. And boy, am I glad that I did. Had I not, I'd have been fighting with a mother over the black eye my daughter gave her son...

What is Mindfulness?

To be cliché, the definition of mindfulness according to the Oxford dictionary is: "A mental state achieved by focusing one's awareness on the present moment, while calmly acknowledging and accepting one's feelings, thoughts, and bodily sensations, used as a therapeutic technique." Being cliché here is okay because I like this definition of mindfulness – it breaks the concept down into a two-step process.

First: focus on the present moment.

Second: acknowledge and accept emotions, thoughts, and sensations.

Mindfulness is an essential skill for children to learn, especially because they can be so easily angered, saddened, and distracted. Just like how my daughter went from exceedingly proud of her castle to being completely ready to wreak havoc on the poor child who unfortunately fell on her fortress. Since I was able to make her mindful of the situation, I was able to avoid the confrontation altogether.

Teaching a child to be mindful from a young age will help them develop mentally, emotionally, and spiritually. Since my daughter has started to practice mindfulness, she doesn't find herself in nearly the same abundance of trouble that she used to get into. Now, she knows to be mindful of situations where her emotions arise quickly.

How Does Mindfulness Work?

Since mindfulness is the process of becoming aware of the current moment and accepting emotions and thoughts that are currently present, it helps you – and your child – take a moment to reevaluate and process the situation at hand. It also helps take the focus away from the emotions and their origination and bring it back onto the present moment by clearing away all those other thoughts. This allows your child to take a moment and think, instead of acting impulsively or rashly.

Looking at it from a different perspective, mindfulness is speeding up the process of emotions. If you're angered, you're going to act on your anger until it dissipates; then when the fog has cleared, you'll think about what happened and allow your rationality to take over and make the next decision from there. The same is true of sad situations. Those can drag out for weeks and months, but once all the crying and heartbreaking has passed, only then can we realize that life moves on, and we should too. With mindfulness, we let ourselves reach the end result without having to wait for the emotions to work themselves out.

Of course, mindfulness can be used in everyday life and it should be, but it may take some time for your child to accept the idea of being aware and present. This book will walk you through the steps to introducing mindfulness to your child,and it will lead you all the way to watching them succeed on their own.

As parents, we know that sometimes there are other challenges to managing life and raising our children, and unfortunately, our children are susceptible to complex problems such as ADHD (attention deficit hyperactivity disorder), anxiety, and OCD (obsessive-compulsive disorder). If your child struggles with a disorder, there are techniques that alleviate some of the problems and stresses that these disorders inflict upon our children. While mindfulness won't be able to replace normal treatment, it could make getting through life a little bit easier for your precious little one.

Maybe your child doesn't have a disorder but he or she simply cannot resist the wonderful satisfaction of sweets, or eating in general, and is constantly shoving food into his or her mouth – be it junk food or otherwise. We all have our weaknesses. I know I absolutely **love** food – sometimes, I have to eat mindfully or I get too greedy. Thankfully, if you teach your child mindful eating, you may be able to give them an essential tool in fighting and winning the battle against their cravings.

"Parents are the ultimate role models for children. Every word, movement and actions has an effect. No other person of outside force has a greater influence on a child than the parent."

Bob Keeshan

2 POISE LIKE A PEACOCK

One of the first principles of teaching your child mindfulness is that you can't set unrealistic expectations for them or their growth. Everyone learns different concepts at varying speeds. Besides, mindfulness isn't a subject that can be taught like addition or spelling. Mindfulness is a concept that will change their life. It will help them in a variety of situations and it will influence their neural development.

For a moment, we'll discuss why setting realistic expectations is important. Children are precious, and when they're young, they will try their hardest to meet our standards, regardless of how high or difficult they are. This can really set them up for strife in their later years. If you continuously push them to become the highest-scoring student in their class, they're going to try their hardest to accomplish that goal.

Just because your child may try to reach your allotted goal, that does not mean they will be able to, and even if they did, it may come with extreme amounts of stress, which is very unhealthy. We may want our children to be the best that they can be, but we cannot forget that they value our approval tremendously.

When dealing with mindfulness, you don't want to express disappointment if your child takes longer than you were hoping to pick up and continue an exercise. These exercises are developing life skills and implementing a change in their routine – it isn't easy or quick to change these things in our lives.

You definitely won't be able to look at it with an all-or-nothing attitude, because your child may make slight progress, and if you give up because they haven't mastered all of it, you're only doing them a disservice. But, I'm sure I don't have to tell you that, I'm just preaching to the choir.

In other words, a peacock doesn't start out with a full throne of colorful feathers. When they are born, they look like a regular bird, but as they grow, their beautiful plumage and feathers appear. While you may know that the bird will turn into a beautiful jewel, you can't get frustrated if it takes a little longer for the feathers to appear.

Next, let's discuss how to help our children meet our expectations. If we set realistic expectations for our children, it's important to let them know the goal we've set for them. It's also important to encourage them and let them know that you'll still love them and be proud of them even if they don't reach the goal quickly, or ever.

Getting to Know the Challenges

Your child will face challenges, that's a fact. What is important is that they know how to overcome those challenges and that you know how to help them. Since there are so many different things your child can face, I've explained a few.

First and foremost, it might be difficult to teach your child how to be mindful at all. They're little roadrunners, and their minds are working incessantly as they learn about the world around them. Children abound with energy and thoughts, so quieting a mind could be the first hurdle to overcome. If your child has ADHD, mindfulness may pose an even bigger challenge, but it will definitely change their life, and it will be worth it in the end. Children who face issues with focusing in general will benefit tremendously from learning to calm their mind and be mindful.

Don't be surprised if your child doesn't want to sit down and learn these techniques, even when you do your best to make them fun and interesting. There will be only so much that they can take. Try to keep in mind your child's attention span and remember to be patient with them as they are learning. Even teenagers report that they find it difficult to quiet their mind and sit still, so this will be a tough challenge for the littler ones, who are constantly awed by every aspect of the world. Each distraction will draw their attention. It will take time and patience. Of course, we're parents, so we know all about patience.

Another common difficulty is that some concepts may be more challenging than your child can grasp at the time. As a child's brain develops, it can master more complex concepts, so if they are having issues learning a technique, it might be a good idea to try a simpler version or a technique for a younger child. Don't worry; this doesn't mean that your little one won't be able to pick up the technique – it just means they need more time.

When trying something new, motivation is important, but we all have trouble motivating ourselves every once in a while. It's a part of our nature, so it should be no surprise if your children become unmotivated in mindfulness, especially if they don't see immediate results. Be their cheerleader and encourage them to keep trying and to stick with it.

Another important point to remember is that you can't use mindfulness as a means of punishment. Every time your child does something wrong or acts on their emotions in a negative manner, you can't assault them with mindfulness, or get onto them about not using mindfulness. It's not something you can force onto them. Deal with the situation like you normally would, and then bring mindfulness into the picture. Ask them how they could have avoided getting in trouble while they were angry. Guide them. Don't try to make them be mindful every time they trespass – that would only work to turn them against the mindfulness exercises.

Monkey See, Monkey Do – Pieces of the Process

This concept is probably not new to you: children like to imitate their parents. Just think of the first time your child heard you say something – maybe it was a bad word – and they repeated it because they wanted to be like you. Of course, if it was a bad word you may have told them that they shouldn't say such things, but that doesn't change the fact that children pick up on everything we say.

We have to be what we want our children to be. If we show our little ones that we practice mindfulness and that it is a part of our own lives, they will want to do it too.

This concept will be useful throughout the book because as you try to teach your children certain techniques, if they see you doing them first, it will help them tremendously.

Let's say it like this: if you were a mother or father peacock and you wanted your chick to walk with poise and

11

grace, you would walk with that exact poise and grace. Then, when you wanted to show them how to spread their feathers, you would spread your own and watch them as they try to imitate you. Your child is a mini you.

Take this opening section as a gentle reminder that all the good practice you undertake with your children will help with mindfulness too. It is also important to mention that it may be wise to start one step at a time – just like when your child was learning to walk. Instead of trying to get them to learn all their techniques right away, try teaching them how to be present with their senses first – I'll walk you through various exercises and give you plenty of tips to get you through this process. Then, teach your child how to be present with their emotions, and eventually you can teach them to accept those feelings. While most guides want you to teach your child how to be present with their emotions and accept them at the same time, I feel it's important to do these separately because acceptance can be difficult, depending on the emotion and the situation. Plus, it may be beneficial to teach discretion with emotions – not all emotions should be accepted and acted upon.

For instance, if Susie is mad at Brad because he accidently kicked dirt on her, she can take a moment to practice mindfulness. Focus on sounds, smells, and other aspects of her current environment that will help her segue into accessing her emotions. She will know that she's angry, but she shouldn't accept and act upon the anger; instead, she should accept that having dirt kicked at her made her angry but that it was an accident, and it does not warrant an angry or aggressive response.

Now that we've covered some basic information, let's get

to what you're looking for, shall we? Don't worry though, if you're itching for more details, the last chapter will cover information about research findings and frequently asked questions, and will also include a short paragraph about how to tailor mindfulness to your child. Spoiler: it's super easy.

"When was the last time you spent a quiet moment just doing nothing – just sitting and looking at the sea, or watching the wind blowing the tree limbs, or waves rippling on a pond, a flickering candle or children playing in the park?"

Ralph Marston

3 STARTING SMALL

Since you're just starting to teach your child mindfulness, it's good to start small. If you begin with the most basic concepts, you'll build a solid foundation that you can continue to build upon. These initial concepts may be frustrating for a teenager who may feel like they should just start with something more challenging, but just like any skill, starting at the beginning is imperative for proper growth, so you may need to convince them that this is the best place to start.

What is the easiest thing to do? Breathe. The very first thing to teach your child in the way of mindfulness is to focus on their breathing. Conscious breathing is essential. If they are having trouble just focusing on breathing and not on other, distracting things as well, then try getting them to inhale and exhale deeply. Get them to take long, slow, deep breaths in and out. Tell them to feel the air fill their lungs, and think about how it feels as it slowly dissipates while they exhale. But of course, don't let them take breaths in a manner that would make them feel light-headed or pass out.

Many researchers, mindfulness practitioners, and even some doctors like to focus on the fundamentals of breathing, especially when teaching mindfulness to a child, because it is the simplest step. So simple in fact, a child does not have to be old enough to understand the word mindfulness to be taught it through breathing.

Teachers, coaches, and parents who have taught children mindfulness have done so by starting with the feeling of breathing, and the sensation of breathing – it's a solid foundation that children can experience and understand. They can feel their lungs fill with air, the momentary pause before exhalation, and then the deflation of the lungs as they breathe out.

Many children will take this small step and run with it, so to speak. Once your child realizes the calming effect that breathing can have, all you have to do is let him or her know that they can always resort back to the breathing technique to calm their mind. It doesn't matter whether they're angry, hurt, scared, or sad, they can always begin to consciously breathe and calm the storm of thoughts.

Another one of the best steps to begin mastering mindfulness is to notice and be aware. No matter how old your child is, getting them to notice things in their environment and to be aware of what is going on is the first step to teaching them mindfulness. Looking at things is easy, but taking notice of things is a little bit more difficult.

As humans, we can only take in so much sensory stimulation at one time. In order to mitigate some of the stimulation, our brains regulate what we notice and what we don't. Things that are old and familiar may not be noticed, while if something is new and irregular, it is more likely to be seen.

Try with your own home as an example. In your living room or bedroom, you may have things lying around that you don't notice or pay any mind to when you go into that room. Maybe it's a pile of junk mail that you sat on the edge of your desk one afternoon and have ignored since then, or perhaps it's the half-empty bottle of shampoo that you forgot to throw away one evening. Items that don't change in any way – especially location – and because they are not very important to our daily lives, they are often overlooked.

Have you ever lost something? You set it down and forgot all about it because your mind didn't bother to notice where you put the item. You mechanically set it down and walked away without being fully aware, which left the information of that item's whereabouts flitting around your short-term memory until it was time to be shredded like an old, useless file.

Since we only take in so much information and we optionally leave things out, taking time out of our day to notice things can be the perfect focus tool that we need to begin our mindfulness journey with our children. In fact, it's the foundation of mindfulness.

Breathing Exercises

For this technique, you want to teach your child about conscious breathing, and that we can breathe differently to fit whatever we are trying to accomplish. We can breathe through our nose or our mouths; we can make our tummies rise and fall, or our chests rise and fall; we can also use a combination, such as breathing in our mouths and out of our noses, or in our noses and out of our mouths.

For Younger Children

Depending on the age of your child, getting them to be interested in *breathing* could be a challenge, or even impossible. Thankfully, there are a few different ways to make the act of breathing in regular air fun and enjoyable for children.

Animalistic Breaths

To get your child interested in what you have in store for them, you may want to use your imagination. For instance, you may want to pretend you're a cow – you take a long, deep breath in, pause, and slowly moo as you breathe out. This can be done with almost any kind of animal sound.

Superheroes

If your child is in love with superheroes, you can let them pretend to be one. If your child loves Superman or Supergirl, for instance, let them take a big breath in – because they're preparing to blow their ice breath all over the enemy – and then, as they breathe out, let them pretend they're freezing their enemies with their powers. If you're standing in front of them, uh-oh! I guess you became frozen too!

This technique also works for dragons breathing out fire. Either way, the children will have a blast being their favorite superhero – plus, it will be a great opportunity to teach them about mitigation of emotions later on. For example: Superman can't save the world if he's mad or sad, he has to take a moment, breathe, gather his senses, and then save the world. If he doesn't, he would want to use his powers recklessly.

Princesses

If your child loves the idea of princesses, an easy and enjoyable way to get them to breathe is to have them pretend they are waking up from a long sleep – like Sleeping Beauty. Their prince has come and rescued them, and now they're taking their first, deep breath in, after being trapped in the glass. To further the imagery, have them sit and stretch out while they breathe in and release a slow, content breath. This would be a great exercise to take even further because if they're a princess waking up from a long sleep, they have to notice all the new things around them that they haven't seen in ages!

Belly Breaths

To get your child to breathe while focused on their tummy, a great exercise is to have them take a deep breath in and pretend that their stomach is full from eating too much – they can walk around holding their tummy and rubbing it, then let the deep breath out slowly, and watch as their tummy disappears.

For Older Children

If your child is older and can stand the idea of breathing in and breathing out without needing their imagination for assistance, then there are several ways to just breath relaxingly.

First, have them just focus on taking deep breaths in, filling the chest, then pause. Hold the breath for a second, and then release it slowly. Ask them to pay attention to how their body releases the breath and seems to relax down. Do this several times. Eventually, they won't be thinking about anything except their breathing.

Breathing exercises are especially useful for children who may suffer from anxiety or ADHD. Breathing during a panic attack is a great way to activate the parasympathetic system – the nervous system responsible for slowing the heart rate, conserving energy, and relaxing. For those with ADHD, breathing is a steady action that helps center the body and contradicts the racing of the mind – when the mind focuses on the solid, steady rhythm, it can be brought back down to a manageable level. But don't worry, if your child has ADHD there will be a ton more exercises that you can practice with them in a future chapter.

Noticing and Awareness Exercises

Noticing and awareness exercises can be quite fun to implement and involve rather easy actions that can be introduced into yours and your child's daily life. The exercises in this section are great for helping your child learn how to experience things in the moment. Being in the present doesn't sound like much but in reality, it means that you're disregarding the haunting of the past, the impending future, and the terrifying "what ifs." When described like that, being present actually sounds pretty amazing – especially for us adults.

If your child is especially anxious or nervous, getting them to practice being present may be a great way to help them mitigate their anxieties. And I think we both know that if their anxieties are lessened, then our own anxieties as parents are lessened. Plus, we'll take less ibuprofen to relieve our headaches!

Thankfully, being present also includes relaxing, so not only does it say goodbye to everything that is anything, but it also says hello to decompression.

It's no mystery that you want your child to grow up healthy, both mentally and physically. But the great part about teaching them to be healthier by being an example is that we're helping ourselves as we help them.

The Basics

Noticing and awareness is all about consciously noticing and being aware of your surroundings – or more pointedly, helping your child become aware and notice things in their surroundings. Although, children are usually very interested in their surrounds. It isn't unusual for them to consistently point things out to us; we're usually the ones who try to stifle all the noticing that they do so we don't have to listen to all the things they see, that we also see.

Getting your child to take notice of the things around them is rather easy, but getting them to notice and focus may pose more of a challenge. Try some of the exercises below and see which ones work best for you and your mini-you.

Younger Children

Playing Sound Detective
If you have access to a computer, this could be a quick and easy exercise for you to practice with your child. Find sounds of drums, guitars or other musical instruments, and have them identify the source of the sound first, and then just listen to the sound of it for ten to fifteen seconds. While this doesn't seem like much, it's a great beginning step for getting your child accustomed to paying attention to their senses and surroundings.

This is a great exercise to do a couple times, but if you overdo it, your child will start to resent having to sit down and listen to boring sounds again and again. Try to do this one – and all of these exercises, really – in moderation.

Walking with Younger Children

While walking is something you can do with your child even if they are older, this version is for the smaller children.

Your young one might be interested in going on an adventure. During your walk, tell your little one to do their best to notice all of the critters that they can find. Use all of their senses. Their ears will point them to birds, dogs, or crickets. They can see the little creepy crawlers on leaves if they look close enough. Maybe they will smell a pond or lake nearby, which will point them to fish or frogs.

When they notice something, give them a moment to enjoy the sense – to see the caterpillar, to pick up the caterpillar (only if it is friendly) – and take a moment to feel the caterpillar crawl across their hand.

I know I don't have to tell you this, but only let them get close to and touch things that you are certain are friendly and won't hurt them.

Doing these little exercises will help your child realize that taking a moment to notice their surroundings will distract them from anything that may be worrying or clouding their mind.

Mindful Raisins

A very common exercise for teaching mindfulness is all about eating a raisin mindfully. It doesn't necessarily have to be a raisin – if your child is opposed to the dried fruit, you could also use chocolate, grapes, or anything really. This is a rather brief exercise because it requires evaluating food and really sensing it throughout the eating process. This activity can be repeated a few times a week.

Often times, this exercise is prefaced with a focused breathing before starting, but that is optional. If done, it will aid in the shifting of focus and relaxation. If it isn't done, then it may be difficult to start the mindfulness eating practice cold turkey.

If you can, simply have your child sit in their chair and breathe in deeply, or if needed, you can use the breathing exercises from above.

Once they've used mindful breathing for a couple of minutes, then you can segue into the practice of mindful eating. Take your food, whether it be a raisin, a piece of chocolate, a grape or anything you like, and instruct your child to look at it. Ask them to take note of the shape, the size, the color, the texture. Once they've got the visual components done, ask them to pick it up. What does it feel like in their hand? How does it feel if it is just ever so gently squished – apply enough pressure to feel it, not enough to bust open the food item.

Have them slowly bring the food to their mouth. What are they feeling? Is their mouth watering? Can they just nearly taste it, despite not having put it in their mouth yet?

Finally, have them put the food into their mouth. What does it taste like? What is the texture? Let them bite into it. Does the flavor change? What does the inside feel like? As they slowly eat the food, ask them to take note of the taste and the texture, how their mouth feels as they eat, how their stomach feels when they swallow, and then refocus on their mouth.

Once they've swallowed the food and taken a moment to be present while eating it, they have finished the exercise.

As a kid, eating mindfully has probably never crossed their minds. They see food and down it goes – as well as all over the place, usually. But mindful eating really brings a focus to something that is mechanical and instinctual, and it can give your child a focus that they lacked before.

Older Children

The Body Scan

This exercise is a rather popular one, and it can be done right before bed or sometime during the day. If your child tends to get stressed before bed or has trouble sleeping, this activity might help them clear their mind enough to sleep. If your child has issues dealing with stresses and emotions during the day, it might be a good idea to get them to do this exercise during the day.

The body scan is an exercise to notice everything about the body and may take a while. To start, have your child lay down. Anywhere safe will do because by changing the surface each time your child lays down, their senses during each session will change, and it will require them to pay attention to a new set of feelings and textures each time.

After your child lays down, make sure their feet are slightly apart, and their palms are facing up. Ask your child to lie as still as possible, and if they need to move, they should pay attention to what is uncomfortable, how they move, and what the new position feels like.

Then, have your child breathe in slowly – listening, feeling, and focusing on their breath in and their exhale. This time, don't ask them to take deep breaths in; instead, they should just pay attention to how they are breathing.

After they've focused on their breath, you can ask them to feel their toes. If they're wearing socks, what do the socks feel like against their skin? If they're wearing shoes, can they feel the inside of their shoes? Are their toes pressing against the toe of the shoes?

Move onto their feet – the tops, the bottoms, and the heels. What does the surface against their heels feel like? Is it carpet? Tile? Grass? Is it cold or warm? Is there a breeze against their feet?

Move to their ankles and legs, and then to their knees. Continue to have them focus on each part of their body as you "scan" your way up. They should notice what their clothing feels like against their skin, if their muscles ache, how the surface they are laying against feels; walk them through anything they could notice.

Go to their thighs, the hips, the tailbone, the butt, the waist, the stomach, the back, the chest, the shoulders, the arms, the elbows, the wrists, the hands (palms and fingers), their neck, and finally their head. They can focus on their chin, nose, eyes, ears, cheeks, forehead, back of the head, and so forth.

Once you've covered every inch of their body, you can ask them to focus on their breathing again, and then have them open their eyes. Since their whole body has been relaxed and idle, it might be a good idea to move slowly into a sitting position. Some younger children may enjoy this exercise, if they can lie still long enough to complete the body scan.

Walking

If you and your child enjoy walking, you two could take a walk around the neighborhood and practice noticing things. Don't limit yourselves to just your vision: try naming sounds, smells, and even textures, if you don't see the object first.

The key to this is not to rush the walk. If you just walk along pointing out the things that you notice, you're not really taking any time for the present, and that won't help you or your child.

If you're both going to point something, out be sure to take time to really sense it. If you notice the birds chirping, stop walking somewhere that's safe to be idle and listen, or just watch the birds flit around for a while. Either way, spend some time and focus on that sense (or multiple senses) in that moment.

If your child is busy experiencing their senses, they won't have the time or focus to worry, stress, or expend energy with other distressing emotions.

Observation

While walking can be a great way to practice mindfulness and get exercise, an alternative for those days you can't get out for a walk is mindful observation. All you need for this exercise is a window, or you could have your kid sit on the stairs and look out at the front or backyard. Simply find a place to sit and observe the world.

Have your child start by taking a deep breath in and clearing their mind. Then, have them notice everything they can see. Encourage them to stay neutral about these objects – don't label them as bad, scary or annoying; similarly, don't label them good either. Remaining neutral while observing simple things is a great building block for the mindfulness practices that will come later.

If your child is looking out the window or sitting on the steps looking at the world, have them notice the colors and textures of what they see instead of identifying it.

For instance, if I'm sitting at a window looking out, instead of noticing that I see a bird, I should notice that it's red and black, small, and fluffy. Instead of looking at the grass, I should focus my attention on the movement of the blades and the different shades of green – or maybe even brown.

Instruct your child not to become enamored with a single item or thing outside. Notice everything, taking time to really see it, and then move on. If your child has problems with distractions or straying thoughts, instruct them to try to notice a new color or shape while they look out the window. The refocusing on a color or shape will push the thoughts from their mind.

Starting small is a great way to introduce your child to mindfulness. It incorporates easy techniques and exercises that allow them to begin the mindfulness development. But how do you get them to continue to practice? You show them that the exercises have value, they accomplish what they're supposed to, and they are important to you. Don't forget, your child values your opinion and wants to imitate what you do – the best way to show them it's important and it matters to you is to do it yourself.

Challenge your child to do a mindfulness exercise three times a day, and slowly increase the number or the type. If you happen to notice that they're being mindful or practicing a mindfulness technique, provide some encouragement and praise. If you really want to reinforce the positive behavior, provide them with a small treat on random occasions when you notice they did their exercises. If they don't know when to expect their reward, it will make it a little more difficult for them to do the exercise just to get an extra cookie.

Those were the building blocks of mindfulness! Let's move on to some more exercises that will help your child build mindfulness with emotions and feelings.

"Motherhood has taught me the meaning of living in the moment and being at peace. Children don't think about yesterday, and they don't think about tomorrow. They just exist in the moment."

Jessalyn Gilsig

4 FEELINGS AND FOCUS

The next step from senses is to consider our feelings and our focus. As adults, emotions can be difficult in almost every form of the word, even though we've had decades to learn how to deal with our own emotions!

Youngsters can have a difficult time with their emotions too. While they're young and don't have as wide a breadth of problems as us adults do, they still have hormones and craziness that they call life. If they're in their early years, they'll be pretty emotional too – just more temperamental, from my experience.

Either way, we can teach our children to manage the two things that we struggle with as adults, so hopefully, they won't have to struggle as much as we do.

Teaching your child how to calm their mind, refocus their attention, and center themselves away from their emotions will help them develop emotional stability during the course of their life. We'll start with exercises that allow them to be present with their feelings. These exercises will help your child develop listening and communication skills that will be useful to express how they feel and accept how others feel too, without judgement. Your child may also learn that their emotions are important to who they are, and that being emotional isn't something that has to hinder them.

As they get used to being present in their emotions, we'll move on to accepting and working through those emotions. As your child grows, they will realize how invaluable this skill will be to them throughout their entire life, and one day, they will thank you. Until then, you'll probably have to listen to them fussing about how they don't want to do what you've allotted for the day.

Psychology researchers praise mindfulness as a great therapeutic practice that will aid your child in developing mentally and emotionally. So let's get into it!

Feeling Exercises

When you're working with your child on their emotions, it's important that you give them a judgement-free zone. If you don't let them know that you aren't going to judge them – get angry with them, punish them, etc. – then your child will be resistant to working with you on these exercises.

Being a parent can be tough; our kids will come to us and cry over a misplaced toy or a dropped cheerio, so sometimes we're used to telling them that it's nothing. We don't want them crying over a dropped cheerio all their life, so of course we'll try to desensitize them to that kind of thing. But during these sessions, we'll have to take a deep breath and hold in our thoughts.

Remember, this is a time for them to learn to feel their emotions. If they expect a negative reaction during your mindfulness practice, it will make them reluctant to share. Be sure not to tell them those things while they're sharing their emotions. We don't want them learning the opposite of what we're trying to teach.

Mindfulness isn't just a tool to get past negative emotions. It allows us – and our children, of course – to relish in our positive emotions, enjoy them thoroughly and really experience them.

If you remember the story I told you in the beginning of this book, my daughter was about to lose her mind at a poor boy who tripped and fell into her sand castle. Of course, she was angry, but I went over to her and practiced mindfulness. We breathed in and out until she was calm again. After that experience, she now knows how to manage her anger and the rest of her emotions. Your child will learn to do the same.

Gratitude Practice

This exercise is a little different than the rest, but multiple sources that teach mindfulness also include a gratitude section. As adults, there are times where we take things for granted, but when those very things are stripped away from us, we regret not taking more time to appreciate them. If we start teaching our children early on to appreciate things, maybe it won't be as much of a regret for them when they're older.

This is a rather easy exercise, and there are tons of different ways to do it. Some people like to give one to three things they are thankful for over dinner, before bed, or just throughout the day.

Sometimes people set a goal of noticing five things that usually go unappreciated throughout the day. For your child, it may be that you did their laundry, or made their bed, maybe a classmate was nice to them at school, or a teacher did something extra.

For your family, try to create a gratitude exercise that you do daily or weekly. This is a great way to introduce mindfulness because we're being mindful of the things we usually take for granted by noticing them. Remember that your child can't be the only one being thankful: monkey see, monkey do!

Also, you and your children or family will realize there are tons of benefits to being grateful. Some studies show that taking time to be grateful can increase happiness and compassion, it can improve self-esteem, increase sleep, and increase productivity and decision making. Wow! And those are only a few of the benefits!

Younger Children

Feels Like What?
Here's another emotion and feeling-related exercise; this one is to guide your child through emotions. Start by asking them what it feels like to be angry, or what it feels like to be happy. Doing this will help them recognize the emotions that they are feeling when they are feeling them.

This exercise walks your child through the different emotions all at once, moving from one emotion to the next instead of focusing on the emotion that they are currently feeling.

A little tip: when you do this exercise, always end on a positive emotion. If your child is currently calm or neutral, encourage them to embrace the positive emotion. It is easy to think about happy things and raise our moods during neutral emotions, but if we're trying to force ourselves to be happy when we are upset we could just dig a deeper hole, and that's not something we want to put on our children.

A variation of this exercise is to have your child sit down and play instrumental music. While they listen, tell them to focus on how the music makes them feel; when it is over, ask them to elaborate.

Mindful Relaxation

This exercise will be a great tool in teaching your child how to relax. While breathing is a great way to get them to calm their mind, it may not get them to completely relax.

For this exercise, your child can either sit down or lay down. If your child has an issue with focusing, a great place to start would be mindful breathing. Once they are able to focus, ask them to relax the various muscles in their body. Maybe you want to encourage them to feel like they are floating on a cloud, or relax so much that their muscles "sink."

Once they are relaxed, have them breathe in and slowly breathe out again. Your child only needs a couple of repetitions to really get themselves relaxed. When their body is relaxed, if their mind starts to stray, they can always refocus on their breathing to help them keep a clear head and a relaxed body. We wouldn't want stressful thoughts to ruin their ability to relax.

Older Children

Self-Compassion

As our children grow older, especially as they enter into middle school and high school, they may find it difficult to appreciate themselves. It's a time of change, of learning, and fitting in. During these years, children want to be like their friends, mimic the crowd, and find a place to fit. Your child may be sensitive to the opinions of others, and this could influence how they feel about themselves, which makes it important to teach them to appreciate themselves early on.

There are several steps to developing self-compassion. To start, instruct your child to put their hand on their heart and take a few breaths in and out. Then, have them think about the last mistake they have made. As they breathe, tell them to forgive themselves. Mistakes are a common occurrence – after all, we're only human. Just because they have made a mistake, it doesn't make them any less of a person, any less lovable, or any less great.

After they have moved past their mistake, ask them to say aloud two things that are great about them, or in other words, their strengths. Instruct them that they should be nice to themselves. Once they are done with this technique, they should do a small task that they enjoy doing, whether it is drawing for a couple minutes or enjoying a piece of candy.

Self-Centering
Often times we can get distracted from who we are by the things that other people want for us, so the best way to remind ourselves who we are is to practice being who we are and being true to ourselves.

This exercise is really simple. After sitting down and taking a few mindful breaths, instruct your child to think about the things that they like to do. Tell them that they shouldn't include things that other people want for them to do, or what other people's opinions are.

For instance, if they like to draw, but every time they think of drawing they remember their art teacher gave them a bad grade, they should be instructed not to think about the bad grade, only the activity that they like to do. If they can't pull their thoughts away from what other people want from them, they should take a moment each time to think about it and remind themselves that it doesn't matter if someone else doesn't like what they do.

If your child wants, they can repeat aloud the things that they enjoy doing, and the things that they believe make up who they are. Comments like, "I like reading and playing basketball," could be something your child enjoys doing. For instance, if your child thinks that their ability to read fast makes them unique or special, you could guide them to say, "I can read fast, and that makes me great." Or, "I read fast, and there is nothing wrong with that."

Active Conversation
This skill is really important for children who don't want to listen to what other people are saying. Active listening involves one person talking about their feelings and emotions and the other listening without trying to think of responses or judging.

To get started on this, it might be helpful if you figure out what you want to talk about before starting the session with your child. It might be wise to keep how your child makes you feel off the list unless it's good and positive things – just don't mention the time they dropped your favorite piece of china. Hopefully, the previous exercise taught them how to stop beating themselves up over it too.

Anyway, once you know what you're going to say, sit down with your child and talk about things. Encourage them to listen without judgement and without thinking about how to respond. Just listen. They can nod their head to show that they are paying attention.

Then, they can talk and focus on what it feels like to talk about things that have an emotional impact on them. They should pay attention to how their body responds to these emotions.

To end the session, instruct your child to take a deep breath, and begin a breathing exercise. You may even want to initiate thoughts of happier things to make sure the mood doesn't linger into the rest of their day.

Accepting Feelings Exercises

Though some of the exercises above might graze on the subject of your child accepting their feelings, this portion is going to cover the topic more thoroughly with exercises intended to help them accept their feelings and deal with them in a healthy manner. As parents, we don't want our children harboring their emotions until they are toxic pools of goo, but we also don't want them exploding because of pent up emotion. Regardless of the age of your child, teaching them to accept and cope with their feelings is always pertinent.

Younger Children

Feeling
For this exercise, sit down with your child and take a moment to ask them how they are feeling. Ask them to identify the emotion they feel and, if there is more than one, do the emotions one at a time. Then, ask them to describe what it's like to have that emotion. For instance, if they are

angry, is it like they are a pot of boiling water? If they are sad, do they feel like the sky about to rain? If they are calm, is it like the seas after a storm?

Let them feel their emotion, but don't fuel it. If they're mad, have them focus on what it feels like to be mad, but not why they are mad. Don't let them fuel the fire of their anger. Have them describe the emotion in different ways – maybe anger is like they will pop, or boil, or like fire. Maybe happiness is like bubbles or splashing in the water.

Ask them what parts of their body respond to the emotion. If they're sad, do their feel it in their chest or their head?

Make sure that you don't respond negatively to any of their emotions, just listen. Let them know they are allowed to feel those emotions. Tell them that all kinds of emotions are normal, and different things will make us feel different ways, and that's okay.

This last part is important for getting them to act appropriately for their emotions: ask them how they should react. Give them examples of how you react to your own emotions. You could say, "When I'm sad, I cry," or, "When I'm mad, I go for a run."

A great little trick for getting younger children to pick up on sympathy is to ask them how they think other people are feeling. If you're out on a walk and you see someone laughing, ask your child what they think that person is feeling and how they know. Then, ask them to describe how that feels.

A variation to this could be that if you see something happen, maybe someone falls down while they are walking, ask your child how they would feel if they fell down. Ask them what they think that person is feeling. Ask them what they would want to happen if they fell down. Would they want someone to help them up? If so, ask them if they should help that person up. Of course, this is just an example, and if that were to happen, they should always be aware of strangers and how dangerous strangers should be, but the concept remains the same.

You could end the exercise by asking your child about how they would feel, and then ask them about how they should deal with that emotion. Doing this would only further the emphasis of accepting their emotions and how to deal with those emotions.

This Then That (for Younger Children)
During this exercise, your child will think about something that made them emotional. It can be a good or bad emotion, or anything in between. Ask them to think about what happened, and encourage them to think about the situation, how it made them feel, and why it made them feel that way.

For instance, if your child was called a nerd in school by someone walking down the hall who saw them with their nose in a book, ask them to think about why it made them sad to be called a nerd. Was it because they felt like they were being made fun of? Was it because they accepted the taunt from another child?

Ask them why being a nerd is a bad thing, and then show them why being a nerd could be a good thing. It means they are smart and they can get good grades. If you show them that there is nothing wrong with being a nerd, and during the exercise they accept that, then ask them how they would feel the next time someone called them a nerd.

The point of this exercise is to walk them through their emotion, understanding why they felt it. Let them know that it's okay to feel that way and they shouldn't suppress their feelings. Then, if needed, ask them to breath mindfully before walking them through the alternatives to the situation and their feelings.

Aside from being called a nerd as a scenario, here is another:

Jeff was upset that Lisa took the last popsicle and he was only given ice cream instead, so he wanted to pull her hair to show how upset he was. Seeing the expression on Jeff's face, his mother steps in. She asks Jeff to think about how Lisa having the last popsicle made him upset. He thinks that he's upset because Lisa got something that he wanted, and he doesn't like not getting what he wants.

Jeff's mom asks him to think about how "we are supposed to get along and be nice to others." She explains to Jeff that Lisa has not done anything wrong, but pulling her hair would be wrong. She then asks him how he could change the situation, and maybe get what he wants. He says that he could ask Lisa if she wanted his ice cream in exchange for her popsicle. If she says yes, they both get what they want. Jeff's mom gently reminds him that if she says no, maybe he should think about how much he likes ice cream, and how thankful he is to have a sweet snack because he could have received nothing while Lisa got a popsicle.

Older Children

Self-Compassion (Expanded)

While you and your child are doing the above-discussed exercise, if you notice that your child is consistent with punishing themselves about even the simplest mistakes, and if you notice that they are sad more times than not, they may be suppressing some emotions and not working through them. If your child is having a hard time with feeling negatively about themselves, encourage them to say, "This is pain." "Pain is a part of being human." And then, "I should love and accept myself."

It doesn't even have to be just sadness; it could be anger as well, maybe they get angry with themselves or others. If they do, it's imperative that they accept their feelings and take time to disarm their emotions – especially if it's something that makes them want to act violently – and then find a way to express the emotion productively. They could even start by saying, "I am angry." "I'm allowed to be angry." "I shouldn't take my anger out on others or myself."

This can be a little difficult because we want our children to be happy all the time, but life isn't easy enough for us or our children to be happy consistently. So while we may want to be motherly or fatherly and take charge of their problem to turn it around for them, sometimes we have to let our children deal with some difficulties on their own.

Of course, we are parents, and we're going to let them know that we love them and care for them, and that if they need us we are here, but we should also give them the tools they need to work through their problems. They are growing

41

into adults, and we need to equip them to face life the best we can.

Another exercise that may help your child work through any issues they may have is this next one.

This Then That

As our children get older, their emotions will get more complicated. While younger children may respond to unfair treatment, older children will have a wider breadth of situations to deal with. They may have a broken romance interest, body images issues, or low self-esteem. If we teach them how to deal with these emotions early on, they'll be ready to face the bigger challenges that life will throw at them.

During this exercise, your child will think about something that made them emotional. It can be a good or bad emotion, or anything in between. Ask them to think about what happened and encourage them to think about the situation, how it made them feel, and why it made them feel that way. Then, ask them to say aloud that they are allowed to feel that way. "I'm allowed to be angry."

Often times we will try to fight our emotions – we will call ourselves stupid and do our best to react oppositely to how we feel because we don't want to feel that way. Accepting our emotions allows us to go with the flow instead of against the flow.

The different with older children, however, is that they should already know how to act differently upon their emotions. They might be angry and be allowed to be angry, but they should do something else with their anger. This is a great opportunity for you as a parent to teach them how to redirect their emotions.

If they're creative and sad, maybe they could create a sad poem, or paint how they feel. Learning to accept our feelings and channel them into different activities is a tremendous step towards having a balanced emotional life.

You have the responsibility to encourage your children to practice these techniques on their own. They are great to do if they are feeling an emotion that is disruptive or overwhelming. If they are so flustered that they can't speak, they should practice mindful breathing and move to one of the exercises that they enjoy and that they think will help.

Once your child starts to implement these strategies into their daily life, they will realize how beneficial they can be and you won't have to remind them to practice mindfulness – while they are at school, they will feel an emotion and remember that a great way to deal with it is through mindfulness exercises.

Now your child knows the fundamentals of becoming present by taking a moment to appreciate the little things in life and discover what is truly around them; they know how to figure out what emotion they are feeling and why they are feeling that way by self-analyzing. This leads to acceptance, but acceptance can't be forced. As parents, we should always be willing to give our children advice on issues if they need it and help them accept their own feelings if they are having difficulties.

It's important to remember that if your child only accepts their emotions but does not express them, it's almost as bad as bottling them up, so finding healthy and productive ways to express emotions with your kid is a great way to teach them how to manage their feelings.

Not expressing your emotions would be as bad as seeing that your body needs a caffeine boost, making your cup of coffee, telling yourself you're going to drink the cup of coffee, and then staring at it in hopes that you'll feel energized. It won't work.

Some of these exercises might be a little difficult to complete, considering as a parent sitting and listening and not acting is against our nature. But remember, we want to equip our children for a successful life. If we always do things for them, they won't learn to do these themselves.

How does that make you feel? And why? What can do you do about it?

"There can be no keener revelation of a society's soul than the way in which it treats its children."

Nelson Mandela

5 MINDFULNESS FOR ADHD

Mindfulness can be used for many different things, and it can help with a plethora of problems and emotions that your child may face throughout life – some common, some uncommon.

While research has shown that almost 80% of participants find some relief from their ADHD while using mindfulness techniques, these exercises should not be used instead of regular treatment, and should only be supplemental if they help. If they do, they should be done in addition to anything your child's doctor has prescribed for them to take or do. Unfortunately, some children battle a much more severe version than others, so these exercises may help some but not others. I hope that your child will be able to find some relief through these methods.

With ADHD, our brains aren't able to focus on a single task, and our neurons fire rapidly for a plethora of different things instead of what we want to focus on. With all of these challenges, simply correcting the problems in our brains before it takes over could aid the challenge of battling these disorders. This is what we propose teaching our children – how to nip it in the bud.

A few of the exercises that we have already covered would definitely be helpful for these challenges, so I'll be sure to point out to you which exercises to try and how they have been altered for children with ADHD, while providing you with a few new ones to use as well.

ADHD Exercises

Younger Children

We all know the challenges of making young ADHD children focus. They just want to vibrate like atomic particles, so getting them to sit still for even a full minute can seem to be an impossible feat. With persistence and patience, they can go from sitting still for just one minute to sitting still for over ten minutes at a time – which of course can be built upon until they can sit still for as long as necessary, but ten minutes is a great stepping stone to longer time periods.

I've heard so many success stories from parents who have tried mindfulness with their children and have been amazed at the leaps and bounds that their child has made. At first, the chances seem dismal – the child will protest, they will be difficult and downright resistant with every fiber of their being – but after some time, they grow to enjoy, look forward to, and prosper in their mindfulness activities. One little girl wasn't able to sit still for more than one minute straight if she wasn't doing something, and after two weeks, she was looking forward to doing her mindfulness exercises and was sitting still for twelve minutes straight!

While sitting still is a great goal, it isn't always possible with our little movers. We have to get them to slow down first, because then we can make them stop.

Slo-Mo
This slow motion exercise can seem strange at first, but I've noticed that it's a wonderful starting point for many of the children that struggle to overcome their constant vibration, so to speak. If your child really likes the gadgets of

villains in their cartoons, they will love this exercise.

For this activity, you and your child are going to have to exercise a little bit of imagination (if you want). Simply start by pretending to zap your child with a "slo-mo ray," a ray that makes them walk in slow motion, and do things in slow motion, whether it's dancing, wiggling and wobbling, or just playing with some toys set aside for this exercise. After you zap them, if they are walking from one side of the room to the other, you should ask them to walk slowly. At first, this should be easy, but within moments your child may feel the urge to move their body quicker. If they are dancing, wiggling or wobbling, they should be careful to keep their balance while they move about freely but slowly. Ask them to focus on how their body feels.

They will get tired of moving slowly, but you should let them know that it is okay to want to move, but right now they should go slow. Encourage them to walk slowly for several paces, even the length of the room, or move slowly for a minute or a few. You may want to move slowly with them, if they don't want to do it without you. Ask them how it feels to move slowly, encourage them to focus on the feelings and sensations their body picks up on. They should "be in the moment" and in tune with their body during this exercise.

If you like, you can "unzap" them and let them move about freely, releasing their energy. In our day-to-day lives, while there are times to be still or slow, there are also times to be active and move about freely the way we want.

If your child is having difficulties with remaining in slow motion mode for too long, see how long is the longest they can practice. Then, encourage them to reach that time each try, and when they are able to reach that time frame, slowly add more time and let them strive to reach a higher goal. It will get easier with time.

For older children who don't want to do silly things, yoga is a great way to move slowly without being "weird."

Freeze

This exercise is not necessarily the step up from the previous exercise, but it could be a good idea to work on the Slo-Mo exercise first, because this one requires your child to be completely still instead of just moving slowly. To start this one, you could pretend to have a freeze ray that you freeze your child with, or you could simply make it a game where, when you say "freeze," they have to stop what they are doing.

This exercise reminds me of the old "red-light, green-light" game from my own childhood. You can have your child walk/run/skip/hop from one side of the room to the other, you can play music while they dance, or you could just ask them to be wiggly and wobbly. After they are active for a little bit, you can "zap" them with your freeze gun or instruct them to freeze.

Variation: Sitting Freeze

For this variation, you should have a chair handy – this will be similar to the game "musical chairs." Ask your child to do anything they want around a chair, and when you say "freeze" they have to sit down and remain still until you let them move again. This one is going to be a little bit more difficult because once they sit they can't move, and that includes fidgeting.

While under normal circumstances your child will be able to fidget in their chair as long as they are quiet, they will be thankful for such a life skill when they get older, because they will know how to calm themselves to the point of stillness and remain that way for several minutes. This could be a great tool for them when they become antsy or unable to sit still.

Tailored Movements Slowed

Does your child have one movement in particular that they constantly do? Maybe they like to bounce their leg, or rub their thighs, rub their hands, jump, pace, etc. – whatever it is, you can bring mindfulness to it. If your child likes to bounce their leg, ask them to do it slower, and ask them how it feels and what's different about it. If they want to go faster, tell them to continue to go slow and to say that it is okay to want to move quicker but that they should remain slow for now. Then, let them speed back up and ask them to focus on how it feels to do it their normal way. Ask them about their muscles, their skin, and their sensory perception in general.

Body Scan

If you've forgotten where this exercise is, it is in chapter three, under "Noticing and Awareness".

If your child can lay still long enough to complete the body scan, you've definitely made some progress! I know it's not easy, even my daughter struggles sometimes! If not, try getting them to complete the two exercises above. It might be a good idea to start with Slo-Mo and then move on to the Freeze exercise. Once they are able to be still long enough, you can walk them through the body scan, and if they are focusing on the body scan instead of the urge to move about, they may be able to complete it, but don't worry if they can't. They will get there; it just takes time and persistence, but I know I don't have to tell you that – that's what being a parent is all about!

To help with the seemingly insatiable need for motion in ADHD children, you may want to do the body scan for each limb and then let them move that limb for a moment before starting up again. For instance, you could scan up through their feet and then let them roll their ankles and move their toes. Then go up through to their hips, and let them move both their legs, and so on.

Older Children

We haven't forgotten about older children – here are some exercises for them too.

Yoga
While this isn't necessarily a typical exercise, yoga can be used as a slow motion exercise to focus on mindful breathing, slow motion/remaining in that position, and attention span. To start, simply find a yoga position or two that you want to practice with your child. Instruct them into that position and maybe even take it up yourself! Make sure to breathe deeply as you ask your child to do the same, and then remain in each yoga position for several deep breaths, or as long as your child can remain in that position. This practice isn't just good for the mind; it will also help with cardio and strength.

During each yoga position, ask your child what they're feeling, how their muscles feel, what is being stretched, and encourage them to remain still in that position if they start to feel antsy. Of course, after they are in a pose for a little while, give them time to release their energy, or use a yoga pose that allows them to be a little more energetic.

Believe it or not, yoga is a proven method to helping children increase their attention span and patience.

Mindful Relaxation

This exercise will be a great tool in teaching your child how to relax. While breathing is a great way to get your child to calm their mind, it may not get them to relax completely, especially if they are being extremely fidgety or full of energy. This exercise is here because regularly getting your child to relax will help increase their attention span and their ability to sit still and it will aid their focus. This is essential with ADHD children, so it has been added to this chapter for your ease of reference.

For this exercise, your child can either sit down or lay down. If your child has an issue with focusing, a great place to start would be mindful breathing. Once they are able to focus, ask them to relax the various muscles in their body. Maybe you want to encourage them to feel like they are floating on a cloud, or to relax so much that their muscles "sink." Ask them to stay like this for several minutes.

If they need to move, you can allow them to get up and shake out some of their energy, but try to get them to sit back down and relax and focus again.

A little tip: be persistent, there will be disruptions. As we know, our children are going to move when we don't want them to, they will "act out" when they aren't supposed to, and they may fall short of the goals, but they will make progress. Just continue to encourage them and work with them. You never want to give up on your child because they will carry that with them for their lives.

Emotional Exercises for ADHD

Once your child has started to master some of the above techniques, there are various other exercises that will help them overcome other challenges associated with ADHD. Studies show that ADHD children tend to battle low self-esteem and other negative emotions, so we can't forget to tailor some of the latter exercises to them too – specifically, the practices that help with noticing emotions and feelings, and then accepting those feelings. Teaching our children that it's okay to feel their emotions and teaching them how to deal with them and redirect them is essential to helping them grow up with a strong emotional intelligence.

My neighbor's boy has ADHD, and as he grew older, there was an obvious amount of self-hatred in him. He was constantly angry with himself and would continuously beat on his head, his thighs, and his arms. His mother did as much as she could for the boy, but the typical medicines weren't working for him, and he suffered each and every day to try to be "normal." After a little while, I asked her if she would allow me to teach mindfulness to her son, while I worked with my daughter. Of course, she was desperate for anything to work and she agreed. After just a few weeks, he stopped beating on his head and would instead take a deep breath and engage in one of his preferred mindfulness exercises.

My neighbor felt like she owed me the world – I received homemade cakes, cookies, and even a pie for about two weeks before I told her that I hadn't done anything special and she didn't need to keep baking me things. Her son just needed a new way to cope with an old problem.

Of course, his mother became interested in mindfulness too, but that's beside the point. That boy was able to find relief from some of his symptoms and manage his disorder better just by learning a few mindfulness tricks. It changed his life. He can appreciate himself now and appreciate life just that much better.

Younger or Older Children

Gratitude and Self-Gratitude
ADHD children are prone to low self-esteem, self-hatred, and low levels of patience for themselves. It's important to expose your child to self-gratitude.

The gratitude exercise is a useful way to encourage your child to see the good things in life and not take them for granted, and that is essential for children to learn at any age! This ultimately will help your child in every aspect of life. Practicing gratitude can improve resilience, encourage relaxation, reduce self-centeredness, reduce materialism, increase optimism, and improve sleep and immune functions. There are so many benefits to practicing gratitude that I can't really see a reason not to. Gratitude could even counteract some of the negative emotions that ADHD subjects children to, and we both know that as a parent you don't want your child facing emotional struggles.

To practice gratitude simply have your child state three to five things that they are grateful for. Then, ask them to state three to five things about themselves that they are grateful for. Finally, have them comment about how they are proud of themselves for overcoming their ADHD in at least one way. Maybe they managed to sit still during class, or remain quiet without fidgeting for longer than usual – whatever it is, they should be encouraged to find pride in their progress and their victories.

Maybe they were grateful that they remembered to do something, or that they are a kind individual, etc. Reminding them some of the good things about themselves will help them fight the low self-esteem associated with ADHD, so this exercise should be done regularly.

This is one of the activities that I insisted my neighbor's boy try. He found it difficult at times and often struggled with being grateful for himself, but even when he was having troubles, I made him sit down and compliment himself. He needed that positive reinforcement.

Wishing Well

The Wishing Well exercise isn't quite putting wishes into wells; instead, it focuses on wishing well for others and for yourself. You should encourage your child to take a moment and close their eyes to do their well-wishing. Once their eyes are closed, begin a breathing exercise of your choice, and after a few repetitious breaths, ask them to wish well for others – anyone they want. They can choose the same people each time or move onto a different set of people with each turn. Once they've wished well for a few people, they should segue to wishing well for their own self. It may be difficult for them to sit still for the entire time, so it might be wise to ask them to start with only two people and then their own self. With time, they will be able to sit still longer and go about this session as they please.

This exercise should be practiced regularly to encourage positive thoughts about themselves and the world around them.

Older Children

Self-Compassion(Altered for ADHD)

As was stated before, ADHD children need to focus a positive attitudes towards themselves. Without this, they could become terribly hateful towards themselves.

There are several steps to developing self-compassion. To start, instruct your child to put their hand on their heart and take a few breaths in and out. Then, have them think about the last mistake they have made. As they breathe, tell them to forgive themselves. Mistakes are a common occurrence – after all, we're only human. Just because they have made a mistake, it doesn't make them any less of a person, any less lovable, or any less great. They should be reminded that having ADHD does not make them any less great or any less lovable. Remind them that ADHD is a part of who they are, and ask them to repeat, "I have ADHD, and that is okay."

After they have moved past their mistake, ask them to say aloud two things that are great about them, or in other words, their strengths. Instruct them that they should be nice to themselves. Once they are done with this technique, they should do a small task that they enjoy doing, whether it is drawing for a couple minutes or enjoying a piece of candy.

Self-Centering

ADHD children need to be centered. With their wandering mind, they may embark on a difficult journey of trying to fulfil their teacher's desire of sitting still, or their tutor's desire of paying attention while she instructs. Either way, ADHD children need to be able to focus on themselves too, without holding themselves to other people's standards.

This exercise is really simple. After sitting down and taking a few mindful breaths through an exercise that will allow your child to calm themselves and their racing mind, instruct your child to think about the things that they like to do. This may be difficult if they go off on tangent thoughts, but just ask them to list things that they like. Tell them that they shouldn't include things that other people want for them to do or what other people's opinions are.

For instance, if they like to run, but every time they think of running they remember their tutor got them in trouble for running when they weren't supposed to, they should be instructed not to think about the reprimand, only the activity that they like to do.

Have your child list the things they like to do and why. Then ask them if there are things that they like to do, but have a hard time doing. If something they like to do is harder because of their ADHD, reassure them that their progress will allow them to do more of what they love.

With continued practice, these exercises should pave the way for your child to have more focus and less jitters, and if you're practicing them with your child, you may find some improvements in your day to day life too! Just be sure to continue to set slightly higher goals each time, and work towards a standard that both you and your child want.

Mindfulness exercises have been the focal point of many

studies lately, and some researchers are considering mindfulness an alternative treatment to ADHD thanks to the substantial benefits that those affected by the disorder can see from regular mindfulness practice.

"The most important thing that parents can teach their children is how to get along without them."

Frank A. Clark

6 MINDFULNESS FOR ANXIETY

Anxiety can be a difficulty burden to overcome, and it can be even more difficult to watch your very own child face such a tremendous, uphill battle. Thankfully, mindfulness can be practiced in a way to reduce anxiety. Not only will it help reduce the number of anxiety attacks that your child faces, but it will also help when practiced at the start of an anxiety attack. Teaching your child to start one of these exercises if they feel an aura of a panic attack could help mitigate a big part of the battle.

A lot of the anxiety exercises are going to focus on the same common principle: grounding. As humans, if we ground ourselves in the here and the now, we can sway our mind from the "what ifs" and "oh goshes."

Our brain dictates everything, so even if we experience the results of an activated sympathetic nervous system, such as those related to an anxiety attack (sweating, trembling hands, frantic breathing, etc.), it's because our brain initiated a fearful state and wasn't able to stabilize itself afterwards.

I want to share a little story with you – one that has to do with an anxious girl. She hated going to school, she hated taking tests, talking with people, and getting lunch in the lunch room. Each and every day, she would get sick to her stomach and beg her mother to keep her home. The anxiety of going to school was making her sick and she couldn't take it. The mother took her daughter to several doctors, and they all came to the same conclusion: it had to be stress. There were no ulcers, no parasites, no excess acid, she didn't have IBS (irritable bowel condition) or anything that the doctors could detect.

Her mother and father tried to do everything they could to reduce her anxiety. Eventually, she received anxiety medications that made it more bearable to attend school, but she never stopped dreading the educational institutions.

One day, her mother stumbled upon some mindfulness solutions on the internet and insisted that her daughter try. Within three weeks, that girl was coping better than she had for months. Every time she started to dread school or began to have a panic attack, she would focus on a mindfulness exercise. She would calm herself down, and then affirm to herself that school was a good place, and that her fears didn't have to control her. Over time, she stopped being so anxious and eventually she was able to enjoy social interactions, make friends, and take leaps and bounds in school. She found out the lunch ladies were rather nice.

As I stated in the beginning of this chapter, working with calming the mind before it goes haywire is a great way to cease and desist before it really becomes a problem. Hopefully, some of these techniques will help your precious child. These exercises have made the difference for many people struggling with anxiety, so let's get to it!

Younger Children

Pop the Balloon
This is another breathing exercise, designed for younger children. Breathing exercises are a magnificent stepping stone to other grounding exercises, so you may want use other activities after this one to calm your child down. Of course, these exercises will be most effective if they are

practiced regularly and then utilized as anxiety occurs.

For this activity, your child is to pretend their belly is a balloon. The ideal position is for your child to be laying down, but sitting in a chair will work as well. Ask them to breath in, pretending that their belly is a balloon; as they breathe in, they are filling the balloon full of air. Then, as they exhale, they can make a balloon-deflating sound. Do this a few times to achieve their full attention. If we teach our children to do this exercise several times, when they have anxiety and go to implement this calming technique, they will instinctively do it several times. If we only taught them to do it once, they would do it just once, and wonder why they haven't calmed down afterwards.

Paper in the Wind
For this exercise, you will need a piece of paper. A piece of notebook paper would probably work, but with a little difficulty, so it might be a good idea to cut it smaller, like the width of a shopping receipt. You could also use a feather or other easily moved objects – a fluffed-up cotton ball or a small flower are just a few ideas. If you have a small three inch by five inch notebook, a piece of paper from there would be perfect. Your child can be standing or sitting for this. When you are both ready, simply hold up the piece of paper or other object – or have your child hold it – and ask them to blow on it. They should see the piece of paper go back and vibrate slightly at the force of the wind. Many other objects will do the same thing. Ask your child to observe the motion of the paper or object.

As they blow onto the paper, ask them to imagine all their troubles, worries, fears, and anxieties being blown out and away from them. Do this a few times, just so that if this method is used during an anxiety attack, your child will be sure to do a few instinctively.

Younger or Older Children

Arm Trace

The Arm Trace exercise is great for younger or older children. While I suspect some younger children won't want to do this exercise, others will benefit from it, so feel free to try it and see if your little one will find it useful.

This exercise helps your child with breathing deeply and grounding when faced with anxiety. To start, have them hold their arm out perpendicular to their body. It doesn't matter if their palm is faced up or down; this exercise will work either way. Instruct your child to put their finger on their wrist. Then, ask them to take a deep breath in, filling their lungs. As they do, they should move their finger towards their elbow. Ask them to focus on the feeling of their finger traveling across their skin as they breathe. Then, have them trace the same line back out to their wrist as they exhale. They should do this several times before stopping, and they should not breathe in and out in a manner that would cause them to become light-headed or pass out.

Perfect Flaws

We want our children to accept that they have anxiety, because if they try to fight it and resist it, it will haunt them for their lifetime. If we can teach them to accept it as a part of who they are, they are more likely to work through it, manage it, and even prosper despite their struggles. So, how do we help them accept their anxiety?

As a parent, it can be difficult watching our child deal

with their battles, but do we tell them that they're allowed to have those battles, and that it's okay. For this activity, simply take a moment with your child and start a breathing exercise. After they've breathed deeply for a minute or two, ask them to close their eyes and just listen. Tell them that it's okay to be anxious and there is nothing wrong with being different. Ask them to repeat, "It's okay to be anxious," as they breathe out. Then, "It's okay to be me," on the next breath.

If your child is older and can handle it, you may want to ask them how some of their triggers make them feel and remind them that it is okay to feel that way. Have a breathing/grounding exercise handy if needed.

Gratitude and Self-Gratitude

These two exercises in the ADHD section will help with your anxious child as well. All children with struggles will need to remember to be thankful and appreciate themselves. If not, they could start resenting themselves for being different.

Wishing Well

Of course, wishing well for self and others is a great tool to lift your child's spirits and remind them that they deserve good things, but so do other people. This exercise is also in the ADHD section.

Older Children

Counting Breaths

This exercise is meant to calm down the sympathetic nervous system before it has a chance to wreak havoc and initiate the panic phase, but it is as simple as breathing. It may also work during an anxiety attack if prompted by you for your child – and if you can get your child to focus on you and your instructions long enough to complete them.

Simply instruct your child to breathe in deeply and count a few seconds as he or she does – preferably between 5-7 seconds. Then, ask them to breathe out and count to 9-11 seconds. If your child breathes in 5 seconds, have them breathe out 9 seconds; 6 seconds in and 10 seconds out, or 7 seconds in and 11 seconds out.

This will help your child be centered. If they are about to have an anxiety attack, it may be hard to get them to focus on breathing and counting, but it very well could calm them down.

Mindful Savoring
This one is really my favorite of the mindful eating exercises, mainly because it gives me a reason to eat cake – who doesn't want a reason to eat something they enjoy? To do this exercise, you can gather something that your child loves to eat, and maybe they love to eat it so much that they just scarf it down every time. A small piece of cake, chocolate, or fruit, if they enjoy eating fruit, or anything really – just a few bites worth is all you need to start.

After the food is out, and your child is nearby, ask them to take a bite, but not to eat it right away. Instead, they need to taste the food and savor it in their mouth. Have them close their eyes and focus on the taste. As they chew, have them inhale and exhale slowly through their nose, letting their body sink down into their chair. While they sink into their chair, they should imagine that all the bad, stressful things are leaving their body. Of course, they should continue to savor the taste as they breathe in, and not let their thoughts detract from savoring their treat.

This exercise will help with grounding, focus, and attention. If we can get our children to pull themselves away from stressful situations or triggers when they first notice the trigger, we can save them some of the anxiety – at least at first.

To be useful, this exercise should be practiced prior to associating it with anxiety in any way. After your child has the hang of it and notices that it takes their mind off what is happening in the current moment, then you can guide them to "step away" when they begin to feel overwhelmed – if possible – and steal themselves away to enjoy a simple treat. Of course, not everyone's anxiety attacks are the same, and pulling away before being drowned in that kind of emotion/physical and physiological response may not always be possible. You just have to see what works for your child.

Hopefully, some or all of these exercises will help your child deal with their anxiety and distresses. They should be practiced regularly to provide the most beneficial results for your precious mini. Some exercises are great as part of a bedtime routine; others could be done a few times a week, and some even less, and then just as needed. However, remember to also do the exercises for a long enough period that they would help with the anxiety, if your child were to start using these exercises on their own.

You may even want to encourage your little one or big one to work on these exercises if they have problems and to use them when they feel they might need them. With time, they will work them up to regular practice.

"There are only two lasting bequests we can hope to give our children. One of these is roots, the other, wings."

Johann Wolfgang von Goethe

7 MINDFULNESS FOR OCD

As I've prefaced before, your child does not have to be facing these issues to use these exercises; they will be helpful to your child's development either way. However, if your child does face one of these challenges, these exercises may help alleviate some of the battle.

Obsessive-compulsive disorder tendencies aren't the end of the world. I say this in good faith because research has shown that mindfulness can be a treatment to OCD. Cognitive behavioral therapy (CBT) is a prime technique used by psychologists and psychiatrists, and it's based on altering the client's cognitive processes to improve their day-to-day life. Even better, there is a mindfulness-based cognitive therapy (MBCT).

We don't have to continue to watch our children obsess over thoughts with no control; we can step in an offer a possible solution to soothe their mind. OCD is an anxiety disorder, and being so, I refer you to the last chapter's anxiety section to complement this section. Reducing their anxiety could help reduce their tendencies, because anxiety can exacerbate obsessive-compulsive behavior.

I'm obliged to let you know that different things work for different people, and these exercises may not be the only thing that your child needs. I also don't recommend or endorse quitting treatments or therapy for these exercises; I simply want to offer a tool to aid in the seemingly uphill battle of helping your child.

With the complexity of this condition, it could seem

almost impossible for something so simple as mindfulness to have such a profound impact on OCD, but there are many strugglers who have professed their new found adoration for mindfulness, simply because it has given them some relief from their symptoms.

One older boy loved his compulsions; they were the security that lulled him to sleep at night. The stove had been checked ten times, the door locked five times, the house paced for any stray objects three times, and all the books on his shelf had been rearranged in the same alphabetic order six times. It was a strange ritual, he admitted, but he knew that once he stopped fighting with his thoughts and carried out these actions, he could fall asleep soundly – only if he did everything.

The nights that he couldn't remember or the nights where he wasn't sure he did everything in the exact order, he started over. The nights where he accidentally brushed his teeth after doing these things, he would repeat them. They had to be the last thing that he did, even if it made his mouth dry.

Eventually, his friend talked him into participating in some mindfulness exercises, and to be sure that he was sticking to them, he did every mindfulness exercise with his OCD-stricken friend.

Through all the doubts, and fighting with the anxiety and all the other turmoil, after about a month, he finally started to see some relief. He was not lucky to see results right away, but after four weeks of doing mindfulness daily, he had grown to rely on it, and he noticed that it had a slight impact on his tendencies.

Eventually, after sticking with it for a while, he found he could give up his nightly routine for a simple mindfulness exercise, and he could go to bed relaxed and calm. If his thoughts start to invade, he partakes in a breathing exercises and falls asleep. He never once thought a nightly routine could be so simple.

OCD Exercises

Younger Children

Guided Imagination

While this exercise may not be obviously helpful, the benefits are sure to come. Guided Imagination allows your child to free themselves of obsessions. Practicing this a few to several times a week may improve your child's ability to deal with their obsessive thoughts. To prepare for this exercise, make sure you find a quiet room in your house. You may want to play gentle background music, preferably without words, which may help drown out the noise and relax your child.

Don't use a script if your child has anxiety, fear, or difficulties with any of the situations mentioned in the Guided Imagination scripts. For instance, if your child hates lakes, don't use the lake script – it will not be relaxing for them, and they will not benefit from it. If your child has obsessive thoughts and compulsive tendencies in relation to going to lakes or bodies of water, their mind may get distracted with their obsession instead of being relaxed. You may want to take a moment to read the scripts prior to completing them with your child – I know you wouldn't want something in the script that you didn't notice to be distressing for your child and then have to stumble around it! As parents, we only want to do the best that we can for our children.

To start, let your child know you are going to take them on a journey and ask them to get into a comfortable position. They can be sitting or lying down, whichever they prefer. Once they are ready, ask them to close their eyes and walk them though a mindful breathing exercise. When they are relaxed, ask them to just listen to your words, then read the following script to them:

Castle Script
"Imagine you're walking through a forest. There are trees all around you, and squirrels are scampering by. You hear the leaves crunch under you, and you hear the sounds of the birds singing. As the wind blows gently against your face, you hear the rustling of the leaves. You've had a long walk, and you're ready for some rest. As you walk ahead, you leave the forest behind and see a giant castle in front of you.

You stop and look at it. It's big and grey. As you draw near, the giant gate comes down for you. You feel like you know this castle, like it is your castle. As you walk through the gate, you enter into a beautiful giant room. Against the wall, there are long stairs. As you step up, you feel like you know this room. It has a big bed, a window facing the forest, and a dresser with a lamp on it. You walk up to the dresser, and you see that it needs a key. As you reach into your pocket, you pull out the key and unlock the drawer. When you open it, you notice a bright green stone on a ring. This is your ring, in your room. You put the ring on your finger, and it is smooth and cold.

You can tell your secret to your ring. You can tell it your

problems, or anything that is troubling you. They can be big or small. When you tell the ring your secrets, it will keep them; when you tell the ring your problems, it will make them disappear. They will be gone.

Take a moment to talk the to the ring. No one else will know what you share with your ring."

Give them a moment to talk to their ring, and then keep reading.

"Once you've told your ring everything, you notice that the bright green rock is turning dark green, and it slowly turns grey. The grey is your problems, your worries, and your fears – everything you've told the ring. Now watch the ring; it stays grey for a moment before turning into the bright green color once again. Your problems are gone now.

You feel free, calm and happy. You're at peace. The ring has taken your problems and made them disappear, turning them into good, happy feelings for you. It doesn't matter what problems you face; if you can't stop thinking about something, if you feel bad, the ring will take those bad things and turn them into good things. Look at the bright green glow from the ring; there is nothing bad left.

You can return the ring to the dresser, and relock the dresser. After you have returned the ring to the dresser, you turn around and walk to the window. From the window, you can see the forest you came from, and you can breathe in the crisp air from outside. You feel at home in this castle.

Now clear your mind and take a deep breath. Breathe out, and open your eyes."

Lake Script

"Imagine you're walking across a field. You can feel the wind blowing gently against you, pulling softly on your clothing. You can feel that you're ready for rest and you see a giant tree standing tall and strong beside a lake.

You stop and look at it. The lake is deep, blue and beautiful beside the tree. As you draw near, you walk into the shade of the tree and sit down against the trunk.

When you look into the water, you see a giant leaf that has been pulled to the edge of the grass. You pick it up from the water and look at it. The leaf is bigger than your hands, and it shines in the sunlight. This is your leaf. You can talk to the leaf under this tree. The tree grew the leaf just for you.

Take a moment to talk the to the leaf. No one else will know what you share."

Give them a moment to talk to their leaf, and then keep reading.

"Once you've told your leaf everything, you notice that the shining green is turning dark grey and brown. The dark colors are your problems, your worries, and your fears – everything you've told the leaf. Now, place the leaf back into the water.

When you do, notice how the lake draws it towards the center. As the leaf gets closer and closer to the center of the lake, you see the color returning, and it becomes a shiny green again.

You feel happy, calm, and free. You have no more

worries. The leaf and the lake have taken your problems and made them disappear, turning them into good, happy feelings for you. It doesn't matter what problems you face, if you can't stop thinking about something, if you feel bad, the leaf will take those bad things and turn them into good things. Look at the bright green of the leaf; there is nothing bad left.

Whenever you want to return to the lake, your leaf will be there, waiting for you. You can always tell it anything. Each and every time, it will make your worries disappear. There is nothing left of them.

Lean against the tree, rest your body. Feel yourself relax. You're free and happy, and you can sit here without bad emotions.

Now, clear your mind and take a deep breath. Breathe out slowly, and open your eyes."

Among the Clouds Script
"Imagine you're walking Along a path with meadow flowers each side. Stop and look closely. See the red poppies on long stalks and the little daisies shrunk amongst the grass. You keep walking and the path begins to gently rise and slope up towards the sky and towards the clouds.

You keep taking steps one after another after another. The air around you becomes misty and the air presses coolly against your skin. Soon you arise out of the foggy air and you are stood on top of the cloud in the greatest expanse of blue.

You step out onto the cushioned surface and sink in but stop and stand on the field of cloud that stretches across the horizon. You continue to walk and feel as if you are hovering above the world like an Angel.

You explore. You see dips and hills and you skim up and down and around. There is a gap in the cloud and you see the glorious earth below – expanse of field and there, in the distance the sea. Stop still for a moment and think: what else can you see?

Time has come to walk down the path to earth. It is where you thought it would be and you feel the change o surface on your feet. You take slow steps through the mist and soon there is the sun and the grass the poppies and the daisies. You feel the breeze on your face and you breathe slowly.

Now, clear your mind and take a deep breath. Breathe out, and open your eyes."

Make your own! If the Guided Imagination exercise is helping your child overall, you may want to consider creating a script of your own that reflects your child's likes and interests. My daughter loves going on a guided imagination trip where she's being a mermaid, or imaging that she is in the mountains – my little snow angel! The trick is to just walk them through the scenery, and then give them something or some way to get rid of their negative emotions. Whether they are putting them on paper and throwing them into the ocean, or they're taking off a garment that has all their worries, fears, and problems, it's up to you. After they get rid of their problems, let them feel okay and relaxed; let them feel like they don't have anything in the world to fret over.

Self-Actualization
This exercise entails helping your child with finding and

asserting themselves. In the mess of life, your child may feel like they don't have control over anything, that the world is chaotic and hopeless. In return, they will feel vulnerable, self-loathing, and they might experience other negative emotions simply because they cannot change the world – they cannot bring order to this world. As parents, that is heart-wrenching. I would never want to see my child go through something like that, but sometimes it is inevitable, so that's why I bring this exercise to you. This may seem similar to some of the previous exercises, but keep in mind that it is tailored to the OCD individuals.

To start Self-Actualization, begin with deep breathing. After your child is relaxed, ask them to describe themselves. Instruct them that they should think of positive or neutral things to say about their self.

You should affirm these statements. Your child will have enough time to degrade themselves at other points in time, so if you remind them what is good about themselves and you are sure to affirm it, this will help them in the long run. While as parents we wish that our children would never have anything bad to say about themselves, it is simply an inevitable aspect of life, and that's why we should equip our precious minis with ways to combat these parts of life.

Ask your child to name just a couple of things that they want to improve upon. If they are extra hard on their self, simply remind them that they are only human, and even their favorite superhero or TV character cannot handle everything all at once. Growth takes time.

Assure them that they are not their disorder. Remind them that they are human, and that emotions, panics, and fear are normal. Tell them that they are not their thoughts; they could even think of themselves as a dark grey cloud in the sky that is their mind, and those dark clouds, like the rest of the white clouds, will pass. They don't have to get caught up in the rain, if they just know to let the dark clouds pass.

This may not be an exercise that will have benefits right away, but over time it may become an activity they look forward to. The constant reassurance that they can overcome their thoughts, that their thoughts don't have to be who they are, and that they can be objective about their obsessions and compulsions can be a great step in healing.

Remember, mindfulness is just another tool in the toolshed to help cultivate the garden, but it won't be the only one necessary to till the soil, plant the plants, water them, and get them to grow.

Allowing children to recognize their obsessions and the grip that their thoughts can take on them is a powerful, fundamental step to healing. Instead of finding themselves stuck in low places, they will be able to redirect their mind to notice their strife and have a new perspective. They could think, "Oh, there are those pesky thoughts again, but that's okay. I don't need them," instead of falling quickly and painfully into a hole.

Finding a way to anchor your child with something that can substitute some of their mental battles is a good way to fend off those terrible compulsions and obsessions. For children who have OCD, it might be a good idea to start with an exercise they can do every morning, and if necessary have one for them to do every night before bed. It doesn't have to be one of the exercises listed here; it can be from the anxiety section, an exercise that will help anchor them, or just one that makes them feel at ease. It may be best to have at least one from the emotional portions, like the Wishing Well activity expanded to include more than just self and a few others; maybe self, a family or friend, a random person, and a less-than-ideal person. Or include a gratitude practice that reminds the child to like their self. You may want to do a few different ones to try to give your child a comprehensive way to battle their OCD.

Older Children

Older children would also benefit from the Self-Actualization exercise, the last exercise before this one in the "Younger Children" section.

Observed Thoughts

This exercise is going to be a little different than the Guided Imagination and the Guided Thoughts exercises. Instead of embarking on a mental journey to help children with their troubles, we're going to ask them to think freely without guidance. This is great for helping your child separate themselves from their thoughts, hopefully providing them with a way to combat the obsession that may strike them – though it will most likely take some practice.

For this activity, your child should start with a breathing exercise. Find one that you want to do with your child before moving on to the rest of the exercise. After you have gotten your child breathing mindfully, ask them to think about what it feels like to be inside their body. Ask them not to think about the negative things; they should remain as positive as possible. After they think about how it feels to be in their body, ask them to be aware of their thoughts.

Once they are aware of their thoughts, they need to be objective and allow their thoughts to flow freely, as though they were just waves in the ocean, without disrupting them, labeling them or categorizing them. Just take notice of the thoughts, let them roll freely. Instruct your child to not follow the thoughts. If the thoughts were branches, they shouldn't be followed to the leaves; instead, just follow the trunk up while acknowledging the branches. If they start to follow their thoughts, ask them to bring their focus back to just letting their thoughts pass.

If they are distressed by their thoughts, ask them to try to stay objective, and remind them that their thoughts are not facts and they are not their thoughts. This exercise is to show that they can separate themselves from their thoughts without having to be actively a part of them.

This may not be an easy exercise and could prove difficult even for adults, so do your best to work with your child. If they can only practice this exercise for a short time, set goals to work for longer periods of time. You may want to start with 5-10 minutes and work your way up with your child.

Guided Thoughts
This exercise could be a great tool to use to disarm the obsessive thoughts that your child is plagued with. If it works for them, it may be a good idea to do this exercise regularly and encourage them to do it on their own if they start to get the overwhelming dread of their impending obsessions. Of course, you don't have to wait until they start their obsessive thoughts to practice this exercise; in fact, it should be practiced prior to being needed.

Start by asking your child to get as comfortable as

possible. Then ask them to take a few deep breaths and slow exhales before you start. Once they are ready, read the following script to them.

"Imagine that you are at the beginning of a road. At the end of the road is your own personal safe haven where you can be calm and relax. How are you feeling right now? Don't answer aloud, just think about it. This is the beginning of the road; the feelings you're feeling are only at the starting line. Start walking down the road, continue taking each step closer to the end of the road. With every step you take, you are drawing closer and closer to the end of the road, to peace.

Visualize yourself taking each step, with each step you lose more and more of your current emotions. As you draw nearer, you are going to gain more of the peace and tranquility. Right now, you can feel your current emotions and sensations slowly slipping away. They are leaving you. Continue to walk down the road and invite the peace in.

You're almost there. You can feel the peace strongly now, invite it in. Accept it. Once you are at your safe haven, take a moment to breathe. Relish the peace, the tranquility.

Listen to my words. Inhale. Wait, pause a moment, and breathe out. Breathe in. Pause a moment, then breathe out. Feel your chest fill with air. Feel the air as you hold onto it, and then the sensation of it leaving your body. Your chest rises, and your chest falls. Think about your feet; relax them. Your legs and your thighs – relax them too. You feel the tension slowly leaving your body. Now, relax your back and your shoulders. Your arms are starting to feel less tense. Release your jaw. Un-squish your eyes. Feel your whole body relaxing.

Take a moment, and notice that you are feeling some relief. Your thoughts will come back; simply take a deep breath, or focus on relaxing your body, then your thoughts will go away. Think about breathing, think about relaxing, think of something else.

Now, relax yourself completely. Breathe in, and breathe out. Notice how your thoughts don't have to control you. You've made great progress. Inhale, and exhale. Once your body is relaxed, we will bring you back.

Imagine once again that you are at the end of the road, in your safe haven. At the start of the road is the calm state. As you walk towards it, you feel yourself becoming more relaxed and calm. Take each step like you did in the beginning. You're getting closer and closer. You're almost there. Take a deep breath. Now you are at the calm state. You are calm, alert, and ready. Now you can open your eyes."

"Having children is my greatest achievement. It was my savior. It switched my focus from the outside to the inside. My children are gifts, they remind me of what's important."

Elle Macpherson

8 MINDFULNESS FOR EATING ISSUES

As I stated before, this section is called Eating Issues because it covers more than just eating disorders – it covers consistent overeating and the inability to say no to food or comfort food. My little girl just cannot say no to double chocolate chip cookies – it was so bad that I had to stop keeping my own favorite cookies in the house. My daughter would whine and cry until she got a cookie but one was not enough, and if I didn't give them to her, she would find ways to get them herself. She would even climb onto the counters when I wasn't looking just to get into the top shelf and pull the cookie jar down.

The first time, when I was naive, I left them out on the counter after giving her one. The rest were gone in just the ten minutes it took for me to return to the kitchen, so I do understand a little bit about children who don't know how to say no to some foods! I am just glad it was only double chocolate chip cookies and nothing more common.

But others who have faced bulimia or binge-eating disorder have also found some relief with mindfulness. A high school girl was once obsessed with fitting into her prom dresses, but there was one problem: she bought them a couple sizes too small. She was convinced that if she was not a size two, she was not pretty enough. Of course, she was already a size four and quite petite.

However, she hated the thought of not fitting into her dress so much that she would fret over every meal, thinking each bite was making her fatter and fatter – so much so that she would never fit into her dress. While she was eating, she would start to hate herself so much that by the time she was done with her meal, she would go throw it all up.

When her mother found out, she told her that she needed to start getting treatment, but her daughter refused. She would try to find ways out of the appointments her mother made. She hated being "treated." She hated thinking that there was something "wrong" with her.

To complement the treatment, the psychologist suggested the mother try some mindfulness exercises with her daughter that focused on her eating habits, her stress, and even some of the obsessive thoughts that clouded her mind while she ate.

With a persistent mother, two weeks later, while continuing her regular treatment, her daughter was starting to eat mindfully. She wouldn't run to the bathroom after every meal, and she was starting to accept her body image.

Her mother replaced her dresses with size fours, and the goal was to reach that size once again. Thankfully, she reached the goal, and hasn't started again with her bulimia since. Now, even after her treatment is completed, she continues to practice mindfulness daily and has expanded from just using it for her eating habits.

Younger or Older Children

Mindful Meals (more of a tip than an exercise)
Before I start with this exercise, I want to point something out. Sometimes, we like to eat while doing other things. We set our child's plate down in front of the television and we let them eat while they watch TV. It

doesn't seem like a big deal until we realize one teeny tiny aspect: how much food can we eat when we watch TV? How does mindless eating affect our eating capacity? As an adult, we know that if we sit down with a whole pack of cookies, a whole family bag of popcorn, or even bag of chips, we could eat the entire thing without even realizing it – just because we are watching TV. If we can eat anything in front of a TV set, our children can shovel down absolutely anything while being sucked into a show of princesses, mermaids, or even toy soldiers.

When you're ready to serve a meal, don't set it down in front of a TV screen – eat with your child, and encourage them to eat slowly. They should smell and taste their food, enjoying it fully. Ask them to name a few things they like about their food. Ask what it smells like to them. If you're okay with them touching their food, ask them what it feels like. Encourage them to take a moment and access how the food makes them feel and if they are still hungry. If you eat with them, it may be a good idea to stop and rest for a moment, assessing whether or not you are satisfied with how much you ate, and not just eating until you are full. If you do this, and your child sees you doing it, they might do it as well, or if they ask you what you're doing, you'll be able to explain to them (or you could just explain it while you're doing it).

Try referring back to the Mindful Savoring exercise from chapter five, the anxiety section, or Mindful Raisins from chapter three. Both of these will help your child refocus their eating habits to be more mindful when they eat. Mindful eating will bring a whole new meaning back to eating, and it will take the fear of body image out of the equation. Or at the least, it will allow your child to deal with the image in a more healthy capacity.

Fleeting Thoughts (Self-Control Exercise)

For this exercise, you will want to have or ask your child to imagine a food that they want. Once they have fully imagined it and want it, or can see it and want it, ask them to close their eyes and think of the desire as fleeting. If your child is younger and needs a little more visual, ask them to imagine the thought is an insect that flies away quickly before they can really catch it. Then, ask them to focus on something else, breathing or relaxing, and put away the food item while their eyes are closed. Either walk them through a breathing exercise or get them to relax. If you want, you may even do a short Guided Imagination session. When you are done, their desire should be dissipated.

Simply let your child know that they don't need the item, and they only want it. They have the ability to say no and make themselves stop wanting it. All they have to do is realize that their desire is temporary, it doesn't need to be fulfilled, and they can do something else to distract themselves from it.

For other eating issues that are caused by stress, see some of the relaxation or anxiety exercises. You may even walk them through Guided Thoughts tailored; as the exercise is now, it is great for pulling your child from their thoughts. If you want to tailor for their eating problem, simply remind them that their body is fine the way it is, and walk them through some of the affirmations made within this chapter.

Three Food Senses

I am not a medical professional, but I have tried mindfulness, and I have seen it work.

To help your child if they have an eating disorder like

bulimia, bringing them away from the fears, disgust, and discontentment while they eat is important. If your child has binge-eating disorder, it may be important to get them to eat mindfully, so they don't continue to eat too much. Your child should feel like he or she can enjoy their food without guilt. They shouldn't be plagued with feelings of being fat while they partake in a meal, and they shouldn't feel like they can only enjoy food while they scarf it down and then have to get rid of it.

To start, have your child sit down for their meal or any food in general. Ask them to really enjoy the food – they should focus on how it smells, how it tastes, how it feels in their mouth. Is it squishy? Soft? Crunchy? As they experience the food, they won't focus on their negative thoughts.

If they do start to stray, ask them to take a few deep breaths and clear their mind. Do a breathing exercise or a grounding exercise of your choice with them. Then, have them repeat, "I will enjoy my food. I will eat without guilt. I don't need to feel bad about eating. Food is essential. I will enjoy my food."

If your child doesn't want to eat moderately, try to have them take a few breaths and become aware of their body, their feeling of hunger or of being full, and tell them that they should let their stomach decide how much to eat, not their brain.

Try to do some of these exercises with them consistently; if it helps them during one meal, it may be wise to do it with them for each meal, and then check in with them after they eat and see how they are doing. Maybe stay with them and distract them – do different exercises that will take their mind away from the pestering thoughts of fulfilling their eating disorder. Practicing Wishing Well or Gratitude and Self-Gratitude exercises could help them feel better about themselves after they eat. It might take some time and some trial and error, but you are sure to find something that will work.

Keep in mind that research has shown that 90% of the people who have eating disorders also have other disorders – generalized anxiety disorder and obsessive-compulsive disorder are just a couple. So equip yourself with anxiety and even some of the OCD exercises to more fully aid your child. I know that you want them to see some relief as much as they want relief. Their suffering is always so painful to witness. Be persistent; all hope is not lost.

Hopefully, with the use of the exercises in this section and the activities in some of the other sections, you can find a combination that will allow your child to be relieved of some of their distresses. OCD and eating disorders can be hard to deal with, but your child will do just fine with a parent that cares as much as you do! Be patient and kind, and watch as your child learns to prosper. But do remember that these exercises are not to replace treatment by a medical professional; these are simple exercises to supplement your child's treatment.

"Always kiss your children goodnight, even if they're already asleep."

H. Jackson Brown Jr.

9 MINDING THE MINDFULNESS

You must feel like a mindfulness guru by now, and your child must be feeling pretty capable! That's awesome. The best part is that even though you've made it to the last chapter, this book will still be useful to you and your child. You can use the various exercises discussed in the book for practically anything. For instance, if your child starts middle school and you realize they spiked in anxiety, even if it isn't generalized anxiety disorder, you can flip on over to the anxiety section and help them with the exercises discussed there! I genuinely hope this book has been as useful for you and your children, as practicing mindfulness has been useful to my daughter and me.

However, we aren't done yet. You'll find some useful ideas in this chapter, like frequently asked questions and information about what the scientific research has revealed about mindfulness. So stick around, grab yourself a cup of coffee – you deserve it – prop your feet up, and relax for the rest of this chapter!

I want to start with letting you know that mindfulness can help alleviate symptoms of those with bipolar disorder, schizophrenia, and even post-traumatic stress disorder (PTSD). If your child is struggling with some mental difficulty, mindfulness implemented and geared towards helping them could be a wonderful addition to their treatment. PTSD used to be categorized as an anxiety disorder, but it is now viewed as a trauma and stress-related disorder, for which Guided Imagination, Guided Thoughts, and even stress-reducing exercises would most likely be beneficial. This book has armed you, an amazingly caring parent, with all the tools you need to support your child, regardless of what they are facing.

Mindfulness can be used for shame, guilt, fear, anger, depression, and any number of emotions. Because mindfulness makes you aware of how you feel and what you're experiencing, it arms you with the ability to work on your problems – or your children's problems – without having to wait for time to heal all.

For instance, if your child is struggling with anger issues, it may be a good idea to walk them through a few of the exercises that teach them to calm themselves. That will bring them to a more rational level, and it will help them think about the situation that angered them – as my daughter did in the story at the beginning of this book.

So don't fret, you have a powerful tool in your hands that you can use to make leaps and bounds in your child's life.

Frequently Asked Questions

1. What is mindfulness meditation?
    Mindful meditation is the act of focusing your mind for a period of time to calmly accept your thoughts, feelings, emotions, and sensations. In reality, mindfulness meditation is just called mindfulness most times, because mindfulness requires meditation to really function.

2. What does mindfulness mean in psychology?
    In psychology, mindfulness is seen as a state of being open and accepting of the present moment, while remaining objective to thoughts and emotions. Psychology states mindfulness is a way to live in the present without fretting about tomorrow, or banging your head because of the past.

It's a way to be in the here and now, relieve stress, and become open and accepting – something that is difficult for most of us to do without a little aid.

3. Why should someone practice mindfulness?

Mindfulness has a plethora of benefits, but the bottom line is it's an all-around health aid. It benefits the brain in development, and the brain is always changing. It helps regulate stress, which produces a hormone called cortisol. If cortisol levels remain too high in the body, it could lead to problems like high blood sugar, weight gain, problems with the immune system, gastrointestinal disorders, and cardiovascular disease. Not only does mindfulness lower stress, but it has positive impacts on your awareness, attention span, and focus. So, really, mindfulness should be practiced to increase your overall quality of life. Those who practice mindfulness see so many more benefits than they would have thought possible.

4. What is mindful yoga/mindfulness in yoga?

Mindfulness in yoga is simply yoga with mindfulness introduced. If you've gone through this book, you'll remember that one of our exercises implanted yoga for older children that deal with ADHD. If you haven't gone through all the exercises yet, you now know where to find it.

However, that wasn't a very good explanation, so here it is detailed out for you: as you practice yoga, you employ the traits of mindfulness. You become more aware of how you feel and how your body feels during your yoga; you become more aware of your surroundings or your thoughts. For instance, you strike a pose and you objectively let your thoughts flow while you pose, or you go into the tree stance and you take a moment to be aware of the sensations in your body. You don't listen to the annoyance that is pulling at your mind, you don't listen to the burning in your thighs; instead, you breathe in deeply and you exhale slowly. You remind yourself that the sweet release of rest will always come after hard work. You are mindful.

The benefits of mindful yoga are two-fold: you get all the mental benefits of mindfulness (relaxation, better focus, etc.), and all the benefits of yoga (healthy exercise, stretching, improved cardio, better muscle performance, etc.).

5. Is mindfulness meditation?

Mindfulness can employ meditation, but sometimes there is mindfulness without meditation. Simply doing exercises that increase your awareness of the here and now and how you are feeling, even to the point of accepting your feelings, can all be done without active meditation. However, many exercises employ meditation as a way of relaxing and segueing into the different aspects of mindfulness. Some would argue that even just looking at a leaf and contemplating it is meditation, but that just boils down to your definition of meditation. If you're not looking and contemplating the leaf as a method of relaxation, and instead are doing it to focus your mind and increase your awareness of the present moment, then in technicality you aren't meditating.

For a technical breakdown – in the Oxford English Dictionary, mindfulness is defined as follows: "A mental state achieved by focusing one's awareness on the present moment, while calmly acknowledging and accepting one's feelings, thoughts, and bodily sensations, used as a therapeutic technique."

In the Oxford English Dictionary, meditation (meditate)

is defined as follows: "Focus one's mind for a period of time, in silence or with the aid of chanting, for religious or spiritual purposes or as a method of relaxation."

Thus, mindfulness is a mental state, and meditation is the act of focusing your mind for a period of time; mindfulness employs meditation. It's hard, almost impossible to have mindfulness without meditation. Meditation can be done without mindfulness, but not the other way around.

6.   What is mindfulness therapy used for?

Good question! And one with a lot of answers too. Mindfulness therapy is used for mental issues such as: anxiety, depression, OCD, ADHD, eating disorders, schizophrenia, bipolar disorder, post-traumatic stress disorder, low self-esteem, and many other things. It is used for health issues such as: high blood pressure, gastrointestinal problems caused by stress, headaches, chronic pain, and many others. Some people just use mindfulness therapy to increase their quality of life – to be more compassionate, thoughtful, and concerned. Some want to be able to let go of their haunting past and look forward to a bright future. Others want to change how they see the world and change how they react to everyday situations. Mindfulness can be used for practically anything.

7.   How to practice mindfulness without meditation?

In reality, mindfulness uses meditation, and saying that exercises of mindfulness don't employ meditation really just boils down to a technicality. If you're adamant about practicing mindfulness without meditation, my advice would be to focus on exercises that don't require you to "focus your mind as a way of relaxation," but you may find that nearly impossible.

8.   Does mindfulness really work?

I want to say that you should try it and find out, or monitor your child after they've practiced mindfulness for a couple of weeks and see the answer for yourself, but I will still take the time to say yes right here. Mindfulness really does work, and it has the backing of hundreds if not thousands of medical professionals and researchers who have started to gather behind the mindfulness motion. Kabat-Zinn elaborated the concept of mindfulness through a research study that changed the lives of those who felt hopeless.

This simple practice has the same results of many over-the-counter and prescription medications, without the nasty side effects. And if you look at the two questions above, you'll see all the benefits to practicing mindfulness. So I would say yes, it really does work.

9.   Is mindfulness cognitive behavioral therapy?

Mindfulness is an aspect of cognitive behavioral therapy. CBT is geared towards changing how you think so that you can make the changes in your life that you want to see. Without some form of mindfulness, CBT wouldn't exist, because you have to be aware of your thoughts and emotions in order to change them. However, there is also mindfulness-based cognitive therapy, which is a cognitive therapy that heavily relies on and utilizes mindfulness to make changes in brain activity and cognitive functions. So yes, mindfulness is cognitive behavioral therapy, but there is more to cognitive behavioral therapy than just mindfulness.

10. Is meditation good for the brain?

Of course! But let me explain: researchers have been studying mindfulness for a while now, and their findings assert that mindfulness and meditation help open up new neural pathways in the brain. The brain will develop with an affiliation for compassion. It also helps increase the size of certain areas of the brain such as the hippocampus – the memory center – and the prefrontal cortex – the area in our brain responsible for executive functions, like planning and decision making – while the amygdala's size decreases – the spot in our brain responsible for initiation the fight or flight response, anxiety and fear.

Not only does the neural pathways open up, but the chemical levels in the brain find an easier balance with meditation and mindfulness. Serotonin, dopamine, and other chemicals are regulated when we practice stress-reducing and uplifting exercises, which is why mindfulness and meditation help with anxiety, depression, and other disorders: the chemical regulation of imbalances in the brain.

11. Does mindfulness lower blood pressure?

In short: yes. Medical professionals, psychological researchers, and scientists in general have found that practicing mindfulness can lower blood pressure. Mindfulness-based stress reduction (MBSR) is the main treatment cited to help lower blood pressure levels in individuals.

To quote Joel W. Hughes, PhD, "Mindfulness-based stress reduction is an increasingly popular practice that has been purported to alleviate stress, treat depression and anxiety, and treat certain health conditions." And he continues with, "Our results provide evidence that MBSR, when added to lifestyle modification advice, may be an appropriate complementary treatment for blood pressure in the prehypertensive range." Thankfully though, prior studies have shown that MSBR can help even in the hypertensive range of high blood pressure. So there you have it, from a medical professional.

12. Does mindfulness aid in falling asleep?

Mindfulness can be used for relaxation, clearing the mind, and reducing anxiety – all things that have to do with sleep. Most people complain about not being able to fall asleep because they are stricken with anxiety – their mind won't stop racing, or they are too stressed. If mindfulness is practiced daily before bed, it can aid in sleep. It could help you and your child, and even the rest of your family, if they too have trouble sleeping.

13. When should I practice mindfulness exercises with my child?

There are several factors that influence the answer to this question. You can practice mindfulness as much or as little as you want with your child. You may want to start with a few times a week if you're just practicing mindfulness simply to increase your child's day-to-day life. Then you can start practicing it daily, and encourage them to implement it as a part of their daily routine. If your child is struggling with ADHD, anxiety, OCD, or some other uphill battle, then you may want to start with at the least once a day, and move to multiple times a day. If your child enjoys doing the mindfulness exercises and they see positive results quickly – not everyone will see results quickly – and want to do them more often, do them as often as they would like, and guide them to do them as much as they want. Mindfulness exercises will only help your child deal with stressors, emotions, and difficult situations throughout the day. Of course, you should also practice mindfulness on your own to show your child it is worth doing.

What Research Shows

Now we're going to get into the juicy part about how mindfulness is this super-awesome, scientifically-proven method for aiding in almost all brain-related matters. Don't believe me? Check out the studies below!

The Start

This book would not be whole if I did not talk about Jon Kabat-Zinn, the pioneer of mindfulness-based stress reduction. In 1979, he offered patients a chance to participate in his MBSR since they were not responding well to the traditional treatments that were being offered.

Effective use of mindfulness courses for anxiety, stress, depression, rumination, fatigue and sleep quality.

In November of 2013, the University of Oxford completed a research study about the effectiveness of an online mindfulness course. After just one month, the participant's stress levels were reduced by 40%, depression levels saw a 57% drop, and anxiety levels were reduced by 58%. The University or Surrey studied the same online mindfulness course and found that it decreased rumination and fatigue and improved the quality of sleep for the participants.

A different study by the Oxford Centre for Mindfulness found that MBCT reduced depressive episodes by 50% over 12 months.

General Benefits

Paul Grossman's meta-analysis of mindfulness-based stress reduction in the Journal of Psychosomatic Research states, "[…] improvements were consistently seen across a spectrum of standardized mental health measures including psychological dimensions of quality of life scales, depression, anxiety, coping style and other affective dimensions of disability. Likewise, similar benefits were also found for health parameters of physical well-being, such as medical symptoms, sensory pain, physical impairment, and functional quality-of-life estimates, although measures of physically oriented measures were less frequently assessed in the studies as a whole." This study was called *Mindfulness-based stress reduction and health benefits. A meta-analysis.*

Through various trials and studies, researchers have recorded findings that show how mindfulness will help with practically anything that occurs in day-to-day life – quality of life, depression anxiety, and other health benefits like pain and physical impairments. But do I really have to tell you that? This whole book has been about how mindfulness is a wonderful tool to improving your life and your child's life. You should of course practice mindfulness so that your child will copy your actions.

Mindfulness and Respiratory Infections
The University of Wisconsin School of Medicine and Health conducted a study showing that people who practice mindfulness will call out sick to work less because of acute respiratory infections. Mindfulness practice also decreases the length of the respiratory infection as well as their severity.

Mindfulness and Sleep
The University of Utah found that mindfulness will help us with our emotional intelligence and emotional management, as well as increasing our ability to sleep at night and improving the sleep quality.

Mindfulness and Binge Eating

Researchers from the University of New Mexico found that mindfulness decreased binge eating.

In several other studies, mindfulness has calmed the minds of participants enough to keep them from feeling the need to binge, and others have developed the habit of eating mindfully, so they eat regularly and moderately instead of binging.

Another study by the Indiana State University and Duke University found that mindfulness decreased brining and depression, while allowing people to enjoy their food without struggling in regards to their control. Mindfulness helped more than just the standard psychoeducational treatment. So, if done right, mindfulness treatments could provide a greater, more pleasant treatment than the psychoeducational treatment. How awesome is that?

Mindfulness and Mental Illness

The University of Oregon conducted a study that found those who practice mindfulness experience changes in their brain that allow them to better ward off mental illnesses, thanks to increased neutral pathways in the brain and an increased myelin sheath around the neural pathways. The myelin sheath is a protective coating that allows signals to travel through the brain quicker.

What Happens When Teachers Use Mindfulness in Their Classroom?

When teachers practice mindfulness with their students, they see improved focus, better emotional regulation, and an increased capacity for compassion.

In 2010, a study showed that elementary students who were introduced to mindfulness had less depressive symptoms in the minority children.

Obviously, children do better in school and socially when they are introduced to mindfulness. You don't have to sit around and let your child be taught by the school, because that may never happen; instead, you can take charge in your own home and teach them mindfulness to see the same results.

Of course, there are more studies than the ones listed here, and there are far more benefits than what is listed here, but this was just a small section to provide you with a little more faith in the process you're using to help your child. I know I enjoy the knowledge that the things I am doing are backed by research, and I'm sure you do as well.

Concluding Thoughts

Remember that mindfulness should be practiced regularly so that your child sees the most benefits from it. Only by practicing with you will your child have the instincts and skills to apply these exercises in difficult moments by themselves. Simply look forward to the wonderful development benefits that your child will see as they grow up. I hope your child enjoys these mindfulness exercises as much as my little girl. I do them with her all the time, and if I start to get too busy in my day, she reminds me!

Mindfulness is a great tool – all you have to do is use it. So what are you waiting for? Compile the exercises you want to use with your child and get to it!

Mindfulness may not be able to solve all your problems, but it will sure put a dent in them!

REFERENCES

Benefits of Mindfulness

Child Mind Institute
https://childmind.org/article/the-power-of-mindfulness/

The Power and Benefits of Mindfulness Meditation | Child Mind Institute
https://childmind.org/article/the-power-of-mindfulness/

Why Teaching Mindfulness Benefits Students' learning
https://ww2.kqed.org/mindshift/2013/09/12/why-teaching-mindfulness-benefits-students-learning/Learning

The 31 Benefits of Gratitude You Didn't Know About: How Gratitude Can Change Your Life
http://happierhuman.com/benefits-of-gratitude/

The Science Behind Gratitude - How to Practice Gratitude - Happify Daily
http://www.happify.com/hd/the-science-behind-gratitude/

How the Brain Changes When You Meditate
https://www.mindful.org/how-the-brain-changes-when-you-meditate/

Seven Ways Meditation Can Actually Change The Brain
https://www.mindful.org/how-the-brain-changes-when-you-meditate/

Mindfulness Meditation Benefits: 20 Reasons Why It's Good For Your Mental And Physical Health
http://www.huffingtonpost.com/2013/04/08/mindfulnes s-meditation-benefits-health_n_3016045.html

Breathing Mindfulness

5 Minute Mindful Breathing Exercise
https://healthypsych.com/5-minute-mindful-breathing-exercise/

Acceptance

5 Steps to Develop Self-Compassion & Overcome Your Inner Critic
https://positivepsychologyprogram.com/self-compassion-5-steps/

Mindfulness for ADHD

Mindfulness Meditation for a Child's ADHD: Natural ADHD Treatment
https://www.additudemag.com/mindfulness-meditation-for-kids-with-adhd/

The ADHD Mindfulness Craze: It all Started with One Little Study - MindfullyADD
http://mindfullyadd.com/adhd-mindfulness-craze/

Mindfulness for Anxiety

3 Mindfulness Exercises to Soothe an Anxious Mind |

Mindfulness Muse
http://www.mindfulnessmuse.com/mindfulness-exercises/3-mindfulness-exercises-to-soothe-an-anxious-mind

How Meditation Helped Me Rein in OCD and Anxiety
http://www.sonima.com/meditation/ocd/

Mindful Eating

Mindful eating - Harvard Health
http://www.health.harvard.edu/staying-healthy/mindful-eating

Research on Mindfulness in Education
http://www.mindfulschools.org/about-mindfulness/research/

So You Think You're Eating Mindfully | Psychology Today
https://www.psychologytoday.com/blog/real-healing/201309/so-you-think-youre-eating-mindfully

Other Information

Fun Mindfulness Activities and Exercises for Children and Teens
https://positivepsychologyprogram.com/mindfulness-for-children-kids-activities/

10 Ways to Teach Mindfulness to Kids
http://leftbrainbuddha.com/10-ways-teach-mindfulness-to-kids/

Panic Attack
https://www.scientificamerican.com/article/what-

happens-in-the-brain-when-we-experience/

22 Mindfulness Exercises, Techniques & Activities For Adults
https://positivepsychologyprogram.com/mindfulness-exercises-techniques-activities/

6 Mindfulness Exercises You Can Try Today – Pocket Mindfulness
https://www.pocketmindfulness.com/6-mindfulness-exercises-you-can-try-today/

Mindfulness-based Meditation: 4 Relaxation Games for Children
http://impactadhd.com/manage-emotions-and-impulses/mindfulness-and-adhd-4-relaxation-games-for-children/

OCD, Mindfulness and Me
https://www.everyday-mindfulness.org/ocd-mindfulness-and-me/

Mindfulness
https://www.psychologytoday.com/basics/mindfulness

Research Studies

Mindfulness Meditation Training
https://www.ncbi.nlm.nih.gov/pmc/articles/PMC4403871/

Cortisol — Its Role in Stress, Inflammation, and Indications for Diet Therapy
http://www.todaysdietitian.com/newarchives/111609p38.shtml

Mindfulness training helps lower blood pressure - Medical News Today

http://www.medicalnewstoday.com/articles/267528.php

Mindfulness Based Cognitive Behavioral Therapy
https://ocdla.com/mindfulness-cbt-ocd-anxiety

Evidence for Mindfulness: A Research Summary for the Corporate Sceptic

https://www.td.org/Publications/Blogs/Science-of-Learning-Blog/2016/03/Evidence-for-Mindfulness

Made in the USA
Lexington, KY
04 April 2018